W9-AMT-037

# Date Rape Drugs

## DRUGS The Straight Facts

## DRUGS
### The Straight Facts

# Date Rape Drugs

### George B. Kehner

Consulting Editor

**David J. Triggle**

University Professor
School of Pharmacy and Pharmaceutical Sciences
State University of New York at Buffalo

**CHELSEA HOUSE**
**P U B L I S H E R S**
A Haights Cross Communications Company
**Philadelphia**

**CHELSEA HOUSE PUBLISHERS**
VP, NEW PRODUCT DEVELOPMENT  Sally Cheney
DIRECTOR OF PRODUCTION  Kim Shinners
CREATIVE MANAGER Takeshi Takahashi
MANUFACTURING MANAGER  Diann Grasse

**Staff for DATE RAPE DRUGS**
EXECUTIVE EDITOR Tara Koellhoffer
ASSOCIATE EDITOR Beth Reger
PRODUCTION EDITOR Noelle Nardone
PHOTO EDITOR Sarah Bloom
SERIES & COVER DESIGNER Terry Mallon
LAYOUT 21st Century Publishing and Communications, Inc.

CONTRIBUTING AUTHOR Alison Donahue Kehner

A Haights Cross Communications ✦ Company

http://www.chelseahouse.com

First Printing

1  3  5  7  9  8  6  4  2

Library of Congress Cataloging-in-Publication Data

Kehner, George B., 1971–
   Date rape drugs / George B. Kehner.
      p. cm.—(Drugs, the straight facts)
Includes bibliographical references and index.
   ISBN 0-7910-7634-2 (hardcover)
1. Date rape drugs—United States. 2. Date rape—United States. I. Title. II. Series.
HV6561.K44 2004
362.883—dc22

                                                              2004011253

All links and web addresses were checked and verified to be correct at the time
of publication. Because of the dynamic nature of the web, some addresses and
links may have changed since publication and may no longer be valid.

# Table of Contents

# The Use and Abuse of Drugs

**The issues associated with drug** use and abuse in contemporary society are vexing subjects, fraught with political agendas and ideals that often obscure essential information that teens need to know to have intelligent discussions about how to best deal with the problems associated with drug use and abuse. *Drugs: The Straight Facts* aims to provide this essential information through straightforward explanations of how an individual drug or group of drugs works in both therapeutic and non-therapeutic conditions; with historical information about the use and abuse of specific drugs; with discussion of drug policies in the United States; and with an ample list of further reading.

From the start, the series uses the word *"drug"* to describe psychoactive substances that are used for medicinal or non-medicinal purposes. Included in this broad category are substances that are legal or illegal. It is worth noting that humans have used many of these substances for hundreds, if not thousands of years. For example, traces of marijuana and cocaine have been found in Egyptian mummies; the use of peyote and Amanita fungi has long been a component of religious ceremonies worldwide; and alcohol production and consumption have been an integral part of many human cultures' social and religious ceremonies. One can speculate about why early human societies chose to use such drugs. Perhaps, anything that could provide relief from the harshness of life—anything that could make the poor conditions and fatigue associated with hard work easier to bear—was considered a welcome tonic. Life was likely to be, according to the seventeenth century English philosopher Thomas Hobbes, *"poor, nasty, brutish and short."* One can also speculate about modern human societies' continued use and abuse of drugs. Whatever the reasons, the consequences of sustained drug use are not insignificant—addiction, overdose, incarceration, and drug wars—and must be dealt with by an informed citizenry.

The problem that faces our society today is how to break

the connection between our demand for drugs and the willingness of largely outside countries to supply this highly profitable trade. This is the same problem we have faced since narcotics and cocaine were outlawed by the Harrison Narcotic Act of 1914, and we have yet to defeat it despite current expenditures of approximately $20 billion per year on "the war on drugs." The first step in meeting any challenge is always an intelligent and informed citizenry. The purpose of this series is to educate our readers so that they can make informed decisions about issues related to drugs and drug abuse.

## SUGGESTED ADDITIONAL READING

David T. Courtwright, *Forces of Habit. Drugs and the Making of the Modern World.* Cambridge, Mass.: Harvard University Press, 2001. David Courtwright is Professor of History at the University of North Florida.

Richard Davenport-Hines, *The Pursuit of Oblivion. A Global History of Narcotics.* New York: Norton, 2002. The author is a professional historian and a member of the Royal Historical Society.

Aldous Huxley, *Brave New World.* New York: Harper & Row, 1932. Huxley's book, written in 1932, paints a picture of a cloned society devoted only to the pursuit of happiness.

David J. Triggle, Ph.D.
University Professor
School of Pharmacy and Pharmaceutical Sciences
State University of New York at Buffalo

# 1

# Introduction

**Although most drugs are developed** with altruistic intentions, sometimes drugs are used for purposes other than what the manufacturer had in mind. Such is the case with the drugs Rohypnol®, gamma hydroxybutyrate (GHB), and ketamine. These drugs were originally developed for specific medical indications, but today are used illegally in drug-facilitated sexual assaults in which unsuspecting victims are incapacitated and left unable to resist sexual advances.

In recent years, drug-facilitated sexual assault has become a growing concern among health and community educators. A number of drugs have become known as "date rape drugs" or "predatory drugs" because they are used to debilitate individuals for the purposes of committing a crime, often sexual assault.

Unfortunately, the use of recreational drugs to commit rape is not a new concept. Alcohol has been used for years to commit rape because of its accessibility, and it is still the most widely used drug for committing sexual assault. The use of other date rape drugs to commit rape is becoming more common, however, because these drugs are easily concealable, inexpensive, and rapid in effectiveness. In addition, they can easily be combined with alcohol to enhance their effects. These date rape drugs are often referred to as "club drugs" because of their popularity in dance clubs and bars. The purpose of this book is to provide the facts about these drugs, in the hope that a better-informed individual can avoid becoming a predator's next victim.

## BACKGROUND

This book identifies and discusses three date rape drugs —Rohypnol®, gamma hydroxybutyrate (GHB), and ketamine— and provides important information concerning each drug's scientific properties, side effects, and legal and illegal uses. In order to understand the properties of these increasingly popular date rape drugs, the concepts of date rape and the sociological impact of date rape drugs must first be reviewed.

Statistical information concerning date rape and its effect on America's younger population is both enlightening and alarming. Understanding the facts and situations associated with sexual assault or rape can help a potential victim become aware of risky situations and/or the signs of date rape drug intoxication.

## RAPE DEFINED AND DEMYSTIFIED

Every state and the federal government treats the act of rape as a crime. Although there are slight variations in the terms used to define the act of rape among the different laws, there is one common element—the victim's lack of consent. An increasingly common and alarming twist on the notion of lack of consent occurs when an assailant uses drugs to commit a rape. In these situations, the victim is incapacitated and is unable to fight off the attacker or is unable to say "no," yet the victim's unconscious state is sufficient to meet the legal definition of rape just as if the victim had expressly stated or demonstrated a lack of consent.

One form of rape often facilitated by the use of incapacitating or intoxicating drugs is termed either "acquaintance rape" or more commonly "date rape." Date rape itself has become increasingly recognized as a real problem in our society. Indeed, the issue came to public attention in the 1990s with the advent of Court TV and the high-profile trials of Mike Tyson and William Kennedy Smith. More recently, basketball star Kobe Bryant has also made headlines in relation to date rape. In all of these celebrity cases, the victims claimed that the defendants, who were known to the victims, forcibly raped them.[1]

The available statistics concerning date rape are a sobering reminder that increased public education about rape is needed. A 1996 National College Women Sexual Victimization Study, funded by the U.S. Department of Justice, found that 20 to 25% of college women are victims of rape or attempted rape during their college careers. In 9 out of 10 cases, the victims knew their perpetrator.[2] A different study conducted by M. P. Koss in 1988 concluded that assailants considered women raped during a date "safe" victims because they were unlikely to view the incident as rape, and, consequently, were less likely to report what happened to the police. The Koss study reported that only 5% of the women raped reported the incident, and more alarmingly, 42% of the victims later had sex with the perpetrator again.[3]

Date rape is most prevalent in the late teens and early twenties age group.[4] A recent study on the subject of date rape reported that women between the ages of 16 and 24 experience rape at rates four times higher than the assault rate for all women.[5] One of the most common myths about date rape is that assailants are readily identifiable as rapists because of their "creepy" character or appearance. In fact, quite the opposite is true. In most cases, college men who were identified as perpe-trators of date rape were viewed by their peers as normal acquaintances or "regular guys" in their daily lives.[6] Sociologists and scientists studying the increased rate of sexual assault and date rape on college campuses point to a number of factors, including certain perpetrator characteristics, victim characteris-tics, and situational considerations (including the use of alcohol and drugs on college campuses), to account for the problem.

## VICTIM CHARACTERISTICS

Though it would be inaccurate to suggest that all victims of date rape fall within a particular category, studies confirm that certain risk factors increase the chances that an individual will become a victim. For example, women who convey a sense of vulnerability or passivity, and who subscribe to "traditional" views that men should occupy a position of dominance over women, may be at risk. One study reported that women who hold such conventional views generally considered date rape excusable or explainable if the woman initiated the date.[7] Similarly, a greater number of women in this category viewed drinking or dressing in a provocative manner as evidence that the rape was the victim's fault in some way.

## PERPETRATOR CHARACTERISTICS

Most college-age men who commit date rape are perceived as "normal," and they believe their behavior is reasonable under the given circumstances. One study found that, while one in 12 males surveyed had committed acts that met the legal definition of rape or attempted rape, 84% of those men believed that what they had done was not rape.[8] Another study asked college-age men whether they would commit a date rape if given an opportunity to do so and get away with it. A whopping 60% of those surveyed responded that they *would* commit rape if they had complete assurance that there would be no negative repercussions.[9]

Just as with common characteristics of victims, there is no "stereotypical rapist." The myth that those who commit rape are obvious rapists, is just that—a myth. In terms of common behavior and attitudes of male rapists, however, there are some typical characteristics. These include the open use of disrespectful speech toward women; engaging in aggressive, hostile, or controlling behavior; and/or believing that the use of force against women is acceptable. Additionally, one article reported a possible link between the level of sexual experience and the likelihood that a man might commit date rape. Those men with a greater amount of sexual experience were placed at a higher risk to become perpetrators.[10] Furthermore, parental neglect and sexual or physical abuse during childhood have been associated with a possible increased risk of becoming a sexual aggressor.[11]

Finally, college-age men who are part of peer groups that tend to accept aggressive behavior are among those most likely to commit gang rapes on campus. Sociologists and psychologists theorize that the powerful male bonding experience that comes from participation in a team sport or fraternity may become the impetus for members of the group to join in the crime with their "brothers" rather than stand alone and do what is right. Membership in a prestigious athletic team or fraternity appears to embolden college-age perpetrators by reinforcing a belief that such behavior is socially acceptable. One study of gang rapes found that in 22 of the 24 reported cases, the perpetrators were members of college fraternities or intercollegiate athletic teams.[12]

## SITUATIONAL CHARACTERISTICS

Although date rapes occur in many settings and under varied circumstances, many, if not most, occur when one of several situational characteristics is present. For example, date rapes largely take place in the evening hours after 6:00 P.M., with most occurring after midnight. The National College Women Sexual Victimization study reported that 52% of rapes occurred between the hours of midnight and 6:00 A.M., 36% occurred between 6:00 P.M. and midnight, and 12% occurred between 6:00 A.M. and 6:00 P.M. In terms of locale, college date rapes occur most often on campus, either in the victim's dorm room, in other housing areas, or in a private room at a party (such as one hosted by a fraternity).[13]

The most significant situational factor is the use of alcohol and/or drugs. The use of intoxicating or incapacitating drugs or alcohol is clearly associated with the occurrence of date rape. Research indicates that in over three-quarters of college date rapes, either the victim, the perpetrator, or both, had consumed alcohol.[14] Alcohol is the most common drug used to incapacitate victims, both because of its ready availability in the youth and college setting and the frequency with which victims ingest it voluntarily at social events. One study found that at least 55% of the victims of date rape had taken drugs or alcohol just prior to the rape, while 75% of the assailants identified in the same study had taken drugs or alcohol just prior to the incident.[15]

Apart from alcohol's incapacitating effects, which impair motor functions and make it more difficult for a victim to resist unwanted advances, alcohol facilitates date rape in less obvious ways. For instance, attackers who ingest alcohol are more likely to misinterpret verbal and nonverbal cues from their victims.[16] Similarly, alcohol also impairs a victim's ability to pick up cues and warning signs that might otherwise give some indication of a potentially dangerous situation.[17] Additionally, when a victim consumes alcohol, it is much more likely that the rape will remain unreported. Many rape victims who themselves have consumed alcohol fear that the authorities will not believe that they were raped, or, worse, will place blame for what happened on the victim rather than the rapist. In the case of date rape, peers are more likely to blame the intoxicated victim for what occurred.[18]

## DATE RAPE DRUGS

Alcohol is just one of many drugs used to facilitate rape. Others include marijuana, cocaine, benzodiazepines, barbiturates, chloral hydrate, methaqualone ("quaaludes"), heroin, morphine, and LSD. Three of the more commonly used drugs today—and the ones that are the focus of this book—are Rohypnol, gamma hydroxybutyrate ("GHB"), and ketamine. Though Rohypnol and GHB were initially used as recreational drugs at clubs and raves, word soon spread among American youth that these drugs could be used quite effectively to commit rape.

This book addresses each of these drugs in detail in the chapters that follow, but their characteristics and properties are worth mentioning here to underscore their dangerous properties. Rohypnol, the trade name for flunitrazepam, is a benzodiazepine similar to Valium®, but it is 10 times more potent. It has many street names, including "roofies," "roache," the "forget-me pill," "ropies," "roach-2," "trip and fall," "mind erasers," and "Mexican Valium." Although it is used as a sleeping pill in some countries, it has never been approved for use in the United States. Rohypnol usually comes in the form of pills that are ingested orally, most often in a drink. After being slipped into the drink, Rohypnol leaves no detectable taste, color, or odor, and will take effect after 15 to 30 minutes. The effects of the drug can be felt for many hours after ingestion. Rohypnol causes visual disturbance, drowsiness, confusion, dizziness, difficulty moving, respiratory depression, and amnesia.

GHB is known on the street as "liquid ecstasy," "liquid X," "grievous bodily harm," "GBH," "Georgia Home Boy," "liquid G," "Somatomax," "Cherry Meth," or "Gamma 10." GHB is a clear, odorless liquid that has a salty taste that can be masked by putting it into a flavored drink. As with Rohypnol, the effects of the drug are felt shortly after ingestion, usually within 15 minutes, and can last for several hours. The effects include decreased inhibitions, drowsiness, deep unresponsive sleep, respiratory arrest, nausea, convulsions, amnesia, and loss of consciousness.

Ketamine is known on the street as "Special K," "vitamin K," or "Lady K." A legal drug sold as a veterinary sedative or hospital-grade anesthetic, ketamine is in the same family of drugs as PCP (phencyclidine). When used in humans, the drug acts as a dissociative anesthetic; it renders the user vaguely aware of, but detached from, all bodily sensations. When taken orally or intranasally (through the nose), the drug takes 10 to 20 minutes to take effect. The most common effects include delirium, vivid hallucinations, cardiac excitement, mild respiratory depression, confusion, irrationality, violent or aggressive behavior, vertigo, ataxia, slurred speech, delayed reaction time, euphoria, altered body image, analgesia, amnesia, and coma.

There are many factors that make these drugs desirable to sexual predators. Because they are, for the most part, tasteless, odorless, and colorless, the drugs are virtually undetectable. All traces of the drugs usually leave the body within 72 hours of ingestion and are not found in any routine toxicology screen or blood test. Therefore, physicians and police have to be looking for the drugs specifically and have to work fast to find them in a victim's system.

Date rape drugs are also used in sexual assaults because they are easily slipped into drinks and are very fast acting. They render the victim unconscious but responsive with little or no memory of what happens while the drug is active in his or her system. The drugs also lead the victim to act without inhibition, often in a sexual or physically affectionate way. Like most drugs of abuse, date rape drugs render a person incapable of thinking clearly or making appropriate decisions. The use of such drugs virtually guarantees a very passive victim, one who is still able to participate in the sex act but who will have little or no recollection of what happened after the event. Without any clear memory of events, the victim is often unaware that he or she has even been raped. Even if the person is aware or has suspicions, those who have been subjected to date rape drugs make very poor witnesses because each of these drugs can cause amnesia while in a victim's system.

## HOW TO TELL IF YOUR DRINK WAS SPIKED WITH A DATE RAPE DRUG

A product that made *Time* magazine's list of best inventions of 2002 is called the "Date Rape Drug Spotter." Developed by the president of Drink Safe Technologies, Francisco Guerra, the product is a simple cardboard drink coaster that can identify two of the most popular date rape drugs: gamma hydroxybutyrate (GHB) and ketamine. A single coaster measures 4 inches by 4 inches and the coasters are designed with two circular test areas located at each bottom corner. Using a swizzle stick, a straw, or even a finger, the user places a drop of the drink onto both test circles and rubs gently. After the area dries, if either circle changes to a darker blue color, it indicates that the drink is contaminated and should be discarded (Figure 1.1).

The coasters are distributed by Guerra's company, located in Wellington, Florida, and are available from some 7-Eleven stores or from the company directly at *www.drinksafetech.com*. Each coaster sells for $0.40 and contains two tests.

In April 2004, another test for the presence of date rape drugs was introduced by British company Bloomsbury Innovations Ltd. It is a test kit with three strips—one for each of the most common date rape drugs. As with the coaster, the user simply takes a sample of his or her drink and places the liquid on the test strip areas. A change in color indicates that the drink contains one of the date rape drugs.

## HOW CAN I LOWER MY RISK?

The best ways to avoid becoming the victim of date rape drugs include several commonsense methods, including the following:

- Watch your drink.

- Watch out for your friends.

- Avoid drinking from punchbowls.

- Do not accept opened drinks; open your own bottle or container.

- Do not trust someone just because she is female; some women have also used these drugs to facilitate date rape.

- Be aware. Awareness is a major factor in this or any other kind of abuse.

**Figure 1.1** The easiest place that a perpetrator can begin to carry out a date rape is at a crowded party or bar. An unsuspecting victim can easily have a drug slipped into his or her drink. The "Date Rape Drug Spotter" is a cardboard drink coaster that can identify two of the most popular date rape drugs: gamma hydroxybutyrate (GHB) and ketamine.

## HOW DO YOU KNOW IF YOU HAVE FALLEN VICTIM TO A DATE RAPE DRUG?

It is difficult, but not impossible, to know if you have been the victim of a date rape drug, even if you don't have access to the test kits. First, there are some very clear signs that sexual activity has taken place even if you have no memory of actually having intercourse. It is important to note that if you have had sex but cannot remember the act itself or recall consenting to sexual contact, you have been raped according to the law. This is true whether a date rape drug has been used or not. Signs that a sexual assault has taken place can include soreness or bruising in the genital area, soreness or bruising in the anal area, bruising on the inner and/or outer thighs, bruising on the wrists and forearms, defensive bruising or scratching (the kind that would occur during a struggle), used condoms near you or in nearby garbage containers, and traces of semen or vaginal fluids on your body, clothes, or nearby furniture. In addition to these physical signs of nonconsensual sex, an extremely reliable sign that you have been raped using a date rape drug is gossip from others about your behavior or the behavior of those around you.

Aside from indications of sexual activity, other clues that you may have been given a date rape drug include feeling "hungover" despite having ingested little or no alcohol, a sense of having had hallucinations or very "real" dreams, fleeting memories of feeling or acting intoxicated despite having taken no drugs or drinking no alcohol, or no clear memory of events during an 8- to 24-hour period, with no known reason for the memory lapse.

Though there are outward indicators to watch for, the reality is that, short of being told that you have been given a date rape drug, there is no way to be sure without medical testing. If you suspect that you have been given a date rape drug, you need to get to a hospital as soon as possible and you must request that you be properly tested. The drugs can be found in your system only if you act quickly.

Awareness is half the battle. If you educate yourself about the science behind date rape drugs, you can better protect yourself from falling prey to someone who exploits these drugs. The next three chapters will discuss each of the three common date rape drugs in greater detail.

# 2

# Rohypnol

Rohypnol is the registered trade name for flunitrazepam, a powerful benzodiazepine. Benzodiazepines are a class of prescription drugs used by physicians as central nervous system depressants. They are commonly known as tranquilizers. Often referred to by street names derived from mispronunciations and misspellings of its name, the drug Rohypnol is often referred to as "roofies," "R-2," "Ro," "rope," "rib," "Mexican Valium," and the "forget-me pill." Because it is the newest drug to be abused by combining it with alcohol, Rohypnol has been called the "quaalude of the 1990s," since quaaludes were popular tranquilizers in the 1960s and 1970s that were abused in combination with alcohol for their sedative and rumored aphrodisiac effects. Abusers often consider Rohypnol the date rape drug of choice.

## HISTORY

Flunitrazepam is a tranquilizer developed in the 1960s by Hoffmann-LaRoche, Inc., and first marketed under the trade name Rohypnol in Switzerland in 1975. It is a member of a class of drugs called the benzodiazepines, which includes drugs such as Librium®, Xanax®, and Valium. This family of sedative-hypnotic drugs is used to treat anxiety, convulsions, muscle tension, and sleep disorders. Rohypnol is a very powerful sedative that can last up to 12 hours, with some residual effects lasting as long as 24 hours. Rohypnol is 10 times more potent than the most commonly known benzodiazepine, Valium (Figure 2.1).

Illicit use of Rohypnol was originally reported in Europe in the late 1970s and worldwide use of it has increased continually since then.

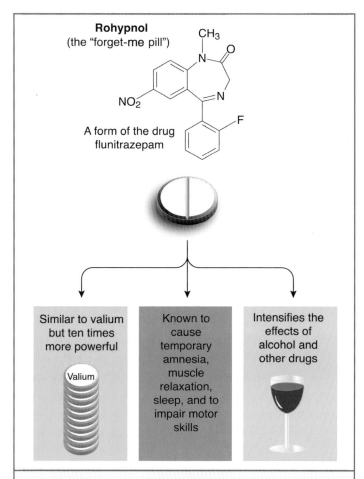

**Rohypnol**
(the "forget-me pill")

CH$_3$

NO$_2$

A form of the drug
flunitrazepam

F

Similar to valium but ten times more powerful

Valium

Known to cause temporary amnesia, muscle relaxation, sleep, and to impair motor skills

Intensifies the effects of alcohol and other drugs

**Figure 2.1** Because of its sedative-hypnotic effects, Rohypnol is often considered the date rape drug of choice. Although it is similar to Valium, it is 10 times stronger. Some of the characteristics of Rohypnol are described here.

Rohypnol was first seen in the United States in the early 1990s in Texas and Florida, as a recreational drug used by both high school and college students. Rohypnol comes in pill form and is usually sold in the manufacturer's original "bubble packaging," which can mislead users in the United States into believing that the drug is safe and legal (Figure 2.2). However, because it is

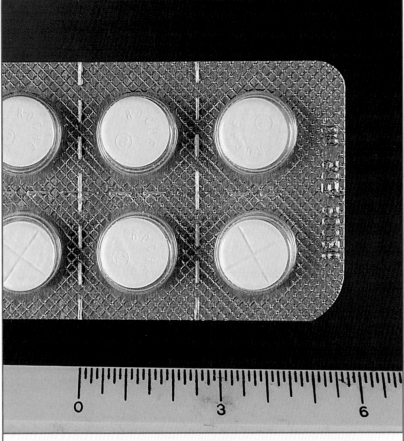

**Figure 2.2** The most common method for packaging Rohypnol tablets and pills is in foil-backed, clear plastic blister packs, as seen in this photograph.

illegal in the United States and is not used by physicians, information on Rohypnol does not appear in the commonly used *Physician's Desk Reference*, a book that contains detailed information about prescription drugs.[19]

Rohypnol is prescribed by physicians and legally marketed in 80 countries in Europe, South America, Africa, the Middle East, and Asia. It is used to treat insomnia, as a preanesthetic medication, and as a sedative-hypnotic. Although Rohypnol

is the most common trade-name product containing flunitrazepam, in many countries it is referred to by additional
generic and trade names. Despite the fact that it is the most
widely prescribed sedative in Europe, Rohypnol has never been
approved for use in the United States because safer drugs are
available.[20] It is abused in every country where it is approved
for sale and marketing. According to the National Institute
on Drug Abuse's Community Epidemiology Work Group
(CEWG), the illicit use of Rohypnol is characterized by its being
taken in conjunction with other drugs, although it may be taken
alone. According to the Drug Enforcement Administration
(DEA), abuse of Rohypnol is most common among heroin and
alcohol abusers. The drug is taken with alcohol or marijuana
to enhance intoxication. Rohypnol also enhances the high or
eases the withdrawal symptoms of heroin, mellows the high of
cocaine, and eases a user down from a crack or cocaine binge.

## PHYSIOLOGICAL EFFECTS

Several agents have the capacity to depress the function of
the central nervous system (CNS) so that calming or drowsiness and sedation are produced. The benzodiazepine class
of sedative-hypnotics has a limited ability to cause profound
and potentially fatal CNS depression. A sedative drug decreases
activity, moderates excitement, and calms the recipient,
whereas a hypnotic drug produces drowsiness and facilitates
the onset and maintenance of a state of sleep that resembles
natural sleep in its electroencephalographic (EEG) characteristics and from which the recipient can be roused easily.
Although coma may occur with very high doses, benzodiazepines cannot induce a state of surgical anesthesia by themselves
and are virtually incapable of causing fatal respiratory failure
or cardiovascular collapse unless other CNS depressants (such
as alcohol) are also present. Because of this measure of safety,
benzodiazepines are generally the medication of choice for the
treatment of insomnia or anxiety.

The introduction of chlordiazepoxide (Librium) into clinical medicine in 1961 ushered in the era of benzodiazepines. Most of the benzodiazepines that have reached the marketplace were selected for their effectiveness as antianxiety agents, not for their ability to depress CNS function. However, all benzodiazepines possess sedative-hypnotic properties to varying degrees; these properties are extensively exploited clinically, especially to facilitate sleep and ease anxiety. Mainly because of their remarkably low capacity to lead to fatal suppression of key CNS functions, the benzodiazepines have displaced barbiturates as sedative-hypnotic agents.

## PHARMACOLOGY

Virtually all effects of the benzodiazepines result from the action of these drugs on the central nervous system. The most prominent of these effects are sedation, hypnosis, decreased anxiety, muscle relaxation, anticonvulsant activity, and anterograde amnesia, in which individuals may experience a loss of memory for events that occurred while under the influence of the drug; events occurring after the drug has worn off are remembered normally.

Rohypnol is a drug that is typically ingested orally but may also be snorted or injected. It has the same general properties as most other benzodiazepines, causing such symptoms as drowsiness, light-headedness, motor incoordination, visual disturbances, gastric distress, impairment of mental and motor functions, confusion, and urinary retention. The main difference between Rohypnol and other benzodiazepines is that it is much more potent. This means that only a small amount of Rohypnol (approximately 1 milligram) must be consumed to experience sedation, whereas a much larger amount of Valium (approximately 10 milligrams) must be consumed to achieve the same level of sedation. After taking Rohypnol, users may feel intoxicated, then sleepy. The feeling is similar to alcohol intoxication, but without a hangover. However, when mixed with alcohol, Rohypnol may cause respiratory depression (a slowing of the breathing rate) that could lead to death.

Rohypnol is available in tablets of 0.5, 1.0, and 2.0 milligrams, although the drug's manufacturer, Hoffmann-LaRoche, phased out the 2-milligram tablet between 1996 and 1999. The manufacturer is currently phasing out the round, white 1-milligram tablet and is replacing it with an olive green, oblong tablet imprinted with the number 542. The new tablet includes a dye that, according to Hoffmann-LaRoche, turns a clear drink blue, a beer green, and a dark drink cloudy. The tablets are packaged in foil-backed, clear plastic blister packs and are sold for $2 to $5 per tablet.[21] A 1 milligram per milliliter injectable solution is also available, but it is not seen often in the United States.

The primary effect of Rohypnol is sedation, which begins about 15 to 30 minutes after ingestion and is experienced as a gradual feeling of drunkenness. Feelings of lessened anxiety and fear are accompanied by a slow, relaxed state of drowsiness, usually leading to sleep or to the user's "passing out." A loss of inhibition can occur, with or without ingestion of alcohol. From an observer's point of view, the user (or victim) appears to be intoxicated, shows a lack of coordination, has bloodshot eyes, and exhibits slurred speech. The effects of Rohypnol peak within 2 hours, but may persist for up to 8 hours or more following a 2-milligram dose. A paradoxical effect of Rohypnol is that, although it is a sedative, it can cause aggressive behavior in some individuals.

The drug is metabolized quickly and is eliminated from the body within 60 to 72 hours after ingestion. Several methods of detecting Rohypnol are now available for sexual assault victims in cases where Rohypnol involvement is suspected. A urine test can detect Rohypnol up to 72 hours after ingestion. A new method is being developed in which a single 2-milligram dose of Rohypnol can be detected in a hair sample up to 28 days after ingestion.[22] Initial studies with this method of detection are promising.

When dissolved in a drink, Rohypnol is odorless, colorless, and tasteless in its original form (as opposed to the new, colored tablets). Even when chewed, the drug tastes mild and not bitter. In an attempt to limit the drug's usefulness for illegal purposes, Hoffmann-LaRoche has reformulated Rohypnol in an attempt to make it easier to detect when it is put into a beverage, as noted above. However, there is still a large stock of the old product on the market. In addition, copy-cat tablets are being produced by pharmaceutical companies in South America and possibly Egypt. These tablets may be reddish-brown instead of white and dissolve well in water. According to the DEA, the product that was seen almost exclusively in the United States up to 2003 was the one manufactured by Hoffmann-LaRoche.

Because Rohypnol is relatively inexpensive, it is popular among high school and college students. In the United States, Rohypnol is used mostly at parties, and although it may be taken alone, it is used most frequently in combination with alcohol. It has a synergistic effect with other sedative drugs such as alcohol, producing decreased inhibition and amnesia. *Synergy* refers to the phenomenon in which one drug increases the effect of another. Among users, Rohypnol is becoming known as a drug "enhancer" because it seems to amplify the effects of many other drugs. Aside from its use as a date rape drug, Rohypnol is used in many combinations. When taken with lysergic acid diethylamine (LSD), Rohypnol can amplify visual hallucinations. It is said to enhance the "high" produced by low-quality heroin and has been used for this purpose in Asia since the early 1980s. Some heroin and cocaine users call Rohypnol a "parachute" drug because it is used to ease the "coming down," or withdrawal symptoms, of the drug-induced high or euphoria.

As with other sedative-hypnotics, repeated use of Rohypnol may result in addiction and physical dependence. Abrupt cessation of the drug can lead to withdrawal symptoms such as anxiety, insomnia, headaches, sore muscles, hallucinations, convulsions, and possibly seizures.

Although overdoses are rarely fatal, emergency services are sometimes required because Rohypnol can cause vomiting, hallucinations, breathing difficulties, and coma. When Rohypnol is combined with alcohol, death is considerably more likely. In addition to monitoring vital signs, emergency room physicians may pump the stomach of an overdose victim to remove any residual contents. An antidote that can be used to reverse the severe sedative effects of Rohypnol (and other benzodiazepine) overdoses is called Romazicon® (flumazenil). It may be administered with careful observation for withdrawal symptoms, such as confusion, agitation, hallucinations, or seizures.

## CELEBRITY OVERDOSE

Very often, the danger associated with drug overdoses does not receive any attention until a celebrity is involved. In 1994, media attention focused on the dangers of overdose caused by the date rape drug Rohypnol. On March 6, 1994, during a concert tour in Rome, rock star Kurt Cobain of the group Nirvana fell into a coma while staying at the five-star Excelsior Hotel. It was revealed that approximately 50 Rohypnol tablets were found in his stomach. He awoke from the coma 20 hours later, and was discharged from the hospital after three days.

Kurt Cobain survived his Rohypnol overdose. The physician who treated Cobain issued the following statement: "Mr. Cobain doesn't know what happened to him. He hasn't gained complete control of his memory. When he emerged from the coma, he was very hungry and asked for a strawberry milkshake!" This quotation demonstrates the amnesic effect of Rohypnol.

## MECHANISM OF ACTION

Rohypnol and the benzodiazepines influence behavior by inter-acting with receptors on neurons in the brain that communicate using the neurotransmitter called gamma-aminobutyric acid (GABA). When GABA binds to receptors, it acts to reduce neuronal activity. Benzodiazepines attach or bind to specific receptors and act by enhancing the effects of GABA. Therefore, benzodiazepines increase or enhance GABA's ability to reduce neuronal activity. Essentially, by further decreasing activity and communication between nerve cells, benzodiazepines cause a depression of CNS activities, such as reduction of anxiety, induction of sleep, and sedation.

## ADDICTION AND TREATMENT

Even though Hoffmann-LaRoche has reformulated Rohypnol tablets to be more easily identified when placed into someone's drink, Rohypnol is still a very potent benzodiazepine and is subject to abuse. Chronic or daily Rohypnol use causes depend-ence in humans. Once dependence has developed, abstention induces withdrawal symptoms, including headache, muscle pain, extreme anxiety, tension, restlessness, confusion, and irritability. Numbness, tingling of the extremities, loss of identity, hallucinations, delirium, convulsions, shock, and cardio-vascular collapse also may occur. Withdrawal seizures can occur in chronic abusers with abrupt cessation of Rohypnol use.

There are more than 30 million people who take benzodi-azepine drugs regularly each year; more than 4 million are addicted. As with other benzodiazepines, treatment for Rohypnol dependence must be gradual, with use tapering off.

## STATISTICS

According to *Pulse Check: Trends in Drug Abuse*, published by the Office of National Drug Control Policy, the availability of Rohypnol appears to be stable at low levels, and the drug is the least available of the club drugs and date rape drugs. The federal government's system to Retrieve Information from Drug Evidence (STRIDE) data show that the number of Rohypnol dosage units seized declined dramatically from 1995 (164,534) to 2000 (4,976) and to 2001 (691).[23]

The National Drug Intelligence Center's 2003 National Drug Threat Survey is a report that draws on information from nearly 2,900 state and local law enforcement agencies as well as from more than 1,000 personal interviews with law enforcement and public health officials. The survey shows that 5.7% of state and local law enforcement agencies nationwide identify Rohypnol availability as high or medium, while 47.4% indicate that availability is low. Another 42.8% of state and local law enforcement agencies nationwide report that Rohypnol is not available at all in their jurisdictions.

Compared to other club drugs, such as Ecstasy, GHB, and ketamine, the use of Rohypnol is at particularly low levels today. According to the National Institute on Drug Abuse's 2002 Monitoring the Future (MTF) study, use of Rohypnol was relatively stable and at low levels between 2001 and 2002 for eighth graders (0.7% in 2001 and 0.3% in 2002) and tenth graders (1.0% in 2001 and 0.7% in 2002). Use for twelfth graders increased from 0.9% in 2001 to 1.6% in 2002; however, the MTF study indicates that data for these years are not comparable because of changes in questionnaire forms.[24]

**TRAFFICKING**

Since the mid-1980s, Rohypnol has been found in the illicit drug traffic of many countries. Studies completed by the World Health Organization (WHO) in 1990 and 1994 revealed at least 35 different countries in Europe, Asia, South America, Africa, and the Middle East in which Rohypnol was sold illegally.

Trafficking of Rohypnol is an international issue. On May 4, 1995, near London, England, police seized 100,000

Rohypnol tablets from a pharmaceutical distributor. This was one of the largest seizures of Rohypnol in history. The investigation revealed that the product had been manufactured in Belgium and was intended for distribution in Egypt.

Because Rohypnol is not manufactured or approved for medical use in the United States, illegal distributors must obtain their supplies from other countries. Colombian traffickers have shipped Rohypnol to the United States via mail services and couriers using commercial airlines. Distributors have also traveled to Mexico to obtain supplies of the drug and then smuggled it into the United States.

Rohypnol abuse and distribution were occasionally reported in the mid- to late 1980s in Florida and in the Mexican border areas of Arizona, California, and Texas, as it was smuggled across the border. Beginning in 1993, the abuse and distribution of Rohypnol began to spread when the number of cases opened by the DEA climbed to 15, most of them in Texas and Florida. The vast majority of Rohypnol-related law enforcement cases occurred between 1993 and 1996. In 1995, the DEA had 38 Rohypnol investigations and recorded the two largest Rohypnol seizures in U.S. history. In February 1995, more than 52,000 tablets were seized in Louisiana and 57,000 were seized in Texas. By March 1996, the DEA had initiated 108 cases, and the U.S. Customs Service had 271 cases. According to the DEA's STRIDE data for 2000, by June 1996, the DEA had documented more than 2,700 federal, state, and local law enforcement cases involving the illegal distribution or possession of Rohypnol.[25]

The most dramatic increases in the distribution of Rohypnol in the United States occurred in Florida and Texas during the 1990s. Between 1990 and 1992, there were 14 state and local law enforcement cases involving Rohypnol in Florida. By 1995, that number had risen to 480, an increase of over 3,000%. Prior to 1994, the cases were located almost exclusively in Miami-Dade County. By 1995, the distribution of Rohypnol had spread throughout the state. Rohypnol was most frequently smuggled into Florida from Latin American countries on commercial airlines.

In Texas, in 1990 and 1991, the DEA documented 8 cases involving Rohypnol. By 1993, the number of cases increased to 169, and by 1995, the number of cases had nearly tripled to 483 and distribution had also spread throughout the state.

Rohypnol was found to have entered Texas by two methods: (1) simple smuggling across the United States–Mexico border, and (2) the abuse of provisions of the Controlled Substances Act of 1970, which permits travelers to carry small amounts of a controlled substance for personal medical use.

Rohypnol is a prime example of an unapproved drug that entered the United States under this medical use exemption. Quantities of Rohypnol and other controlled drugs were carried from Mexico across the border after being declared to the U.S. Customs Service. In mid-1995, a three-week survey at the Laredo, Texas, footbridge disclosed that 101,700 Rohypnol tablets were declared on 796 of the 1,678 declarations filed with U.S. Customs and subsequently entered the United States legally.[26]

The Controlled Substances Act created a series of schedules that established varying degrees of control over substances (Figure 2.3). Rohypnol was placed in Schedule IV of the Controlled Substances Act in 1983 in order to comply with international conventions stemming from the 1971 United Nations (UN) Convention on Psychotropic Substances, although Rohypnol was (and still is) not approved for use in the United States. At that time, there was no known abuse of Rohypnol in the United States. However, in the mid-1990s, the DEA began to consider the merits of transferring Rohypnol to a different schedule. Schedule IV drugs, including Valium and other prescribed tranquilizers, are described as having a currently accepted medical use and a low potential for

---

### Controlled Substances Act—Formal Scheduling

**Schedule I**—The drug has a high potential for abuse, is not currently accepted for medical use in treatment in the United States, and lacks accepted levels of safety for use under medical supervision.

**Schedule II**—The drug has a high potential for abuse, is currently accepted for medical use in treatment in the United States, and may lead to severe psychological or physical dependence.

**Schedule III**—The drug has less potential for abuse than drugs in Schedule I and II categories, is currently accepted for medical use in treatment in the United States, and may lead to moderate or low physical dependence or high psychological dependence.

**Schedule IV**—The drug has low potential for abuse relative to other drugs, is currently accepted for medical use in treatment in the United States, and may lead to limited physical dependence or psychological dependence relative to drugs in Schedule III.

**Schedule V**—The drug has a low potential for abuse relative to drugs in Schedule IV, is currently accepted for medical use in treatment in the United States, and may lead to limited physical or psychological dependence relative to drugs in Schedule IV.

---

**Figure 2.3** This table explains the formal scheduling of drugs according to the Controlled Substances Act of 1970. Drugs are classified based upon their medical uses and potential for abuse. Although some states list Rohypnol in Schedule I, the federal government currently places the drug in Schedule IV.

abuse compared to the drugs or substances in Schedule III. When a drug is placed in Schedule I, more severe punishment is imposed on those caught trafficking the illegal drug. At the state level, Rohypnol already has been reclassified as a Schedule I substance in Florida, Idaho, Minnesota, New Hampshire, New Mexico, North Dakota, Oklahoma, and Pennsylvania. A Schedule I drug has no currently accepted medical use, has a high potential for abuse, and lacks accepted levels of safety for use under medical supervision. Heroin and LSD are examples of other Schedule I drugs.

In the mid-1990s, the DEA proceeded with the administrative scheduling process, as required under the Controlled Substances Act, and submitted its data on the abuse and trafficking of flunitrazepam to the Department of Health and Human Services (DHHS) in April 1996. After scientific and medical review, the DHHS provided its scheduling recommendation to the DEA. It stated that Rohypnol had no accepted medical use in the United States (consistent with Schedule I placement) but that its abuse potential was no different from that of other benzodiazepines, a finding consistent with Schedule IV. In light of this recommendation by the DHHS, the DEA concluded that it did not have sufficient grounds to reschedule Rohypnol. Therefore, the control status of Rohypnol has not changed; it remains on Schedule IV.[27]

Although the scheduling of Rohypnol did not change, the DEA did take other measures to curb the trafficking of Rohypnol. It changed certain regulations that drastically reduced the amount and number of controlled substances that may enter the United States for personal medical use. In 1995, DEA officials met with officials from the U.S. Customs Service and the Food and Drug Administration (FDA) to address the loophole that allowed travelers to carry Rohypnol for personal use. The officials determined that, based on provisions of the Food, Drug, and Cosmetic Act, customs officers could prohibit the importation of Rohypnol. This action by the DEA was meant to prevent Rohypnol abuse from reaching the epidemic proportions that have been seen with other drugs such as crack cocaine and methamphetamine (speed). Although Rohypnol still remains on Schedule IV (even though it is not approved by the FDA for human consumption, is not available by prescription, and is illegal to possess in the United States), U.S. Customs Service officers will seize even small quantities coming across U.S. borders—even those with valid prescriptions from other countries.

## CASE REPORT
## Introduction

Reports of abuse on many college campuses include stories of women waking up naked in unfamiliar surroundings with no memory of the preceding hours. They may have been sexually assaulted but have no memory of what took place. It is important to note that both men and women can be victims of sexual assault, although the vast majority of cases are reported by females. Rohypnol can have an equally incapacitating effect on males. Both males and females have the right to seek treatment after sexual assault and/or suspected Rohypnol abuse.

### Case #1

A 22-year-old female college student was brought to the emergency room by her roommate. She responded to questions slowly; displayed a lack of muscle tone (hypotonia), poor coordination, and slurred speech; and smelled of alcohol. She was initially confused and mildly agitated.

All of the patient's vital signs were found to be normal and she did not have a fever. During the time that her clothing was being removed, she was resistant; she repeatedly grabbed at her clothes and attempted to cover her body.

The patient and her roommate provided the following history: The patient had been out with her girlfriends at a local bar and had consumed a total of four alcoholic beverages during a five-hour period, which was her usual intake once a week. She had socialized at the bar, and her drink had been unattended at times throughout the night. Toward the end of the evening, she began to feel "lightheaded and strange" and accepted a ride home from a male friend. While in the car, the patient began to feel overwhelmingly sleepy. She tried to shake off the feeling but was unsuccessful. When she arrived home, her roommate stated that she was "mumbling and stumbling" and had passed out. Although she had been drinking alcohol, the degree of impairment was unusual for her.

Results of the physical examination were normal and unremarkable. Laboratory tests detected only alcohol in her urine toxicology screen.

After further questioning, the last thing the woman recalled was being approached by a tall man with long black hair, who leaned over to introduce himself to her on the darkened dance floor at the bar. What started out as innocent dancing quickly progressed into the man's attempt to escort the woman out of the bar. Fortunately, a male friend intervened and took the victim home.

The physician discussed with the patient the possibility that a surreptitious drug had contributed to the symptoms she had experienced that night. Although results of the standard toxicological screen were negative, the physician treating the patient believed she may have been a victim of the date rape drug Rohypnol.

Several days after the incident, the patient had pieced together what happened, combining pieces of her own memory and her roommate's recollections. Shortly after the victim met the man with the long hair, she began to act "wasted and drunk," even though she had consumed little alcohol that night. The victim thought the man must have spiked her drink with a Rohypnol tablet when he leaned close to her to introduce himself.

Rohypnol was suspected in this case because of the sudden onset and potent, alcohol-like effects. The degree of drunkenness and disorientation could not have been due to the alcohol alone. The victim had no way of detecting the odorless and colorless pill that quickly dissolved in her drink.

Case adapted from "The Minnesota Daily," University of Minnesota, October 17, 1996. Available online at *http://www.mndaily.com.*

# 3

# Gamma Hydroxybutyrate (GHB)

Gamma hydroxybutyrate (GHB) is an illicitly marketed substance that has long been popular among bodybuilders because of its supposed effect as a strength enhancer. Recently, however, GHB has become popular with teenagers and college-age youth as a drug of abuse (Figure 3.1). The past decade has seen a dramatic increase in the use of GHB and related substances, mostly because of its properties as an aphrodisiac and euphoriant (a drug that enhances emotions or one's sense of well-being).[28] As a result of GHB's current popularity as a recreational drug and its unfortunate effectiveness as a date rape drug, law enforcement officials and forensic scientists are being called upon with increasing frequency to determine the role of these compounds in overdose and sexual assault cases.

## HISTORY

In 1961, a French researcher named Dr. Henri Laborit was the first to synthesize GHB. Laborit was investigating the role of gamma-aminobutyric acid (GABA), an inhibitory neurotransmitter, in the brain. GABA itself does not cross the blood-brain barrier. In synthesizing GHB, Laborit was attempting to create a GABA-like agent that would be able to enter the brain. GHB was shown to

| Common Street Names for GHB | |
|---|---|
| Blue nitro | Liquid E |
| Cherry fx bombs | Liquid Ecstasy |
| Cherry meth | Liquid X |
| Everclear | Longevity |
| EZ Lay | Natural sleep-500 |
| G | Nature's Quaalude |
| Gamma G | Organic Quaalude |
| Gamma Oh | Oxy-sleep |
| Georgia homeboy | Remforce |
| G.H. revitalizer | Revivarant |
| Gib | Salty water |
| Goops | Scoop |
| Great hormones at bedtime | Soap |
| Grievous bodily harm | Somatomax PM |
| G-riffic | Somsanit |
| Growth hormone booster | Vita-G |
| Insom-X | Water |
| Invigorate | Wolfies |
| Lemon fx drops | Zonked |

**Figure 3.1** GHB has many common street names. These are some of the most popular slang terms for the drug.

cross the blood-brain barrier, where some of it was metabolized into GABA.[29]

In 1963, GHB was found to occur naturally in many mammalian cells, including those in the brain. Since that time, it has been purported to act as a neurotransmitter. GHB is both a precursor and metabolite of GABA, although it does not act directly on GABA receptor sites. Recently, a putative GHB receptor has been cloned. This means it may be possible that some of GHB's pharmacological effects could also be due to the activation of a new GHB receptor.

Since its synthesis, GHB has been studied by numerous researchers and has been shown to exhibit a range of effects beyond what was originally expected from a GABA-like compound. In the 1970s, GHB was used as a treatment for insomnia and narcolepsy (a sleeping disorder characterized by involuntary daytime sleep episodes). In the 1980s, body-builders began to purchase GHB at health-food stores because some experts believed GHB promoted muscle growth and fat reduction by increasing the secretion of growth hormone.

In Europe, GHB is available by prescription and has come to be used as a general anesthetic, as an aid in child-birth (increasing the strength of contractions, decreasing pain, and increasing dilation of the cervix), and as a treat-ment for alcoholism and alcohol withdrawal syndrome. GHB came to the attention of authorities as a drug of abuse in the late 1980s. On November 8, 1990, the FDA banned over-the-counter sales of GHB in the United States, after several poisonings in California were associated with GHB overdose. Over the last 10 years, GHB has become widely used as a drug of abuse associated with "raves," or all-night dance parties, and with date rape. However, in 2002, GHB was approved by the FDA as a medication for use in a small population of patients with sleep disorders. It can be pre-scribed by physicians to reduce the number of attacks of cataplexy—a sudden, temporary loss of muscle tone experi-enced by narcolepsy patients.

## PHARMACOLOGY

GHB is available in both a sodium- and potassium-salt form. The sodium salt of GHB is more widely available. Two related chemicals—gamma butyrolactone and 1,4-butanediol (1,4-BD)—are used as equivalents to GHB. GHB is readily manufactured from a precursor, gamma butyrolactone (GBL). GBL is a chemical found in some floor-cleaning products, nail polish, and superglue removers. GHB is created by combining GBL with a strong base, such as sodium hydroxide (a substance with a high pH, commonly known as lye). These substances chemically react to form the unique compound GHB. However, the procedure is very dangerous, and reports have shown that users who make GHB in their own homes frequently suffer caustic burns from the improper dissolution of lye in the chemical reaction needed to produce the drug.

Aside from GBL, another GHB precursor chemical, known as 1,4-butanediol, is used extensively in chemical manufacturing. In 2001, it was estimated that the industrial consumption of 1,4-butanediol in the United States would be 387,000 metric tons.[30] Though its major legitimate uses are in the synthesis of other chemicals, it is also an abused recreational drug. Consumption of both GBL and 1,4-BD can cause the same effects as those of GHB, since they are converted in the body into the active drug.[31] For this reason, both GBL and 1,4-BD sales are regulated.

GHB is ingested orally and is absorbed rapidly from the gastrointestinal (GI) tract. In eight healthy human volunteers, GHB was given in single oral doses of 12.5, 25, and 50 milligrams per kilogram in syrup form. The drug reached its highest blood levels in 25, 30, and 45 minutes, respectively.[32] In a study of six narcolepsy patients taking two 3-gram doses of GHB powder dissolved in water 4 hours apart, the mean peak serum concentrations occurred in 40 and 35.7 minutes, respectively. Because of its rapid metabolism, GHB's pharmacological effects last no more than 3 hours, although (as with any drug), GHB's effects can be indefinitely prolonged by taking repeated doses.

The standard recreational dose of GHB is between 1 and 3 grams, though some people take as much as 4 to 5 grams in a single dose, especially those users who have developed a tolerance. Unfortunately, GHB is most frequently found in a liquid form of widely variable concentration. GHB is a highly soluble drug; 1 gram of GHB powder can be dissolved in as little as 1 milliliter of water, which can make 5 grams per teaspoon (almost 5 milliliters). There is virtually no way to determine the concentration of GHB once it is in liquid form, and, regardless of the amount ingested, the body metabolizes GHB at a constant rate per hour (in the same way that the body metabolizes alcohol). Therefore, even small overdoses can result in temporarily unrousable sleep. When purchased at a club, GHB is generally sold for a few dollars per dose. However, when bought in larger quantities, it is available for $10 to $50 per 100 grams.

## MECHANISM OF ACTION

Like Rohypnol, GHB is a central nervous system (CNS) depressant, which, when tested on animals, induces a sleep-like state in doses ranging from 0.1 to 1.5 milligrams per kilogram.[33] Although many neurotransmitter systems are affected by treatment with GHB, evidence supports the hypothesis that GHB itself acts as a neurotransmitter. This implies that GHB is a naturally occurring chemical in the body that is necessary for normal nervous system functions. Administered as a drug, GHB has been shown to temporarily inhibit the release of dopamine in the brain.[34] This inhibition is followed by a marked increase in the release of both dopamine and naturally occurring opioids, such as endorphins.[35]

The mechanism by which GHB affects dopamine in the central nervous system is unclear. Scientists believe, however, that GHB binds to a possible, yet thus far unidentified, GHB receptor in the brain or to a GABA receptor. It is also possible that GHB is metabolized by the liver and converted to GABA (although this seems unlikely), or that GHB administration triggers the release of GABA, which, in turn, activates the GABA receptor.

Both the GHB and GABA receptor systems have been shown to be inhibitory in nature, meaning that increasing activation of these receptors reduces the activity of the central nervous system. This inhibitory mechanism of action explains many of GHB's physiological effects, such as induction of sleep, inhibition of breathing, and coma. It also explains why GHB can be so dangerous in combination with other drugs—including alcohol, benzodiazepines, barbiturates, and sedatives—that also act by inhibiting CNS activity.

GHB also stimulates pituitary growth hormone release. One Japanese study of six healthy adult men (26 to 40 years of age) reported 9- and 16-fold increases in growth hormone 30 and 60 minutes after intravenous administration of 2.5 grams of GHB.[36] Growth hormone levels were still 7-fold higher than baseline after 120 minutes. The mechanism by which GHB stimulates growth hormone release is not known. Dopamine activity in the hypothalamus stimulates pituitary release of growth hormone, but GHB inhibits dopamine release while it stimulates growth hormone release. This suggests that GHB's growth-hormone-releasing effects take place through an entirely different mechanism. It is likely that the question of how exactly GHB acts on the body will remain unanswered until the GHB receptor is isolated and sequenced, and its properties are better understood.

## PHYSIOLOGICAL EFFECTS

GHB is an intoxicating chemical that is used for recreational, criminal, and medical uses. Users report that GHB induces a state of relaxation and tranquillity. Frequently reported effects include placidity, mild euphoria, and a tendency to verbalize. Users say that anxieties and inhibitions tend to dissolve into a feeling of emotional warmth, well-being, and drowsiness.

Sensations of mild numbing and pleasant disinhibition may also be experienced. At higher recreational doses, effects can include combativeness, dizziness, difficulty focusing the eyes, slurring of speech, nausea, and grogginess. Although its effects have been likened to those of alcohol, the morning after, or hangover, effects of GHB lack the unpleasant or debilitating characteristics associated with alcohol use. In fact, many users report feeling particularly refreshed, even energized, the day after use.[37]

As doses taken are increased, users may experience vomiting, the loss of bladder control, temporary amnesia, and sleepwalking. Seizures, cardiopulmonary depression, and coma have been observed at some of the highest recreational doses reported.

The difference between a high recreational dose and an overdose can be very small. The lethal dose is estimated at perhaps only five times the intoxicating dosage.[38] Furthermore, the drug has synergistic effects with alcohol and likely with other CNS depressant drugs as well. Therefore, small increases in the amount ingested may lead to significant intensification of the effects. Users who drink alcohol, which impairs judgment and with which synergy is likely, are at greatest risk.

The unpleasant and dangerous overdose effect of GHB, which causes temporarily unrousable sleep or coma, occurs at a dose just slightly higher than that which is considered recreational. Thus, a GHB user who hopes to get a "high" can easily ingest enough of the drug to produce serious long-lasting and undesired effects. The effects of GHB are dose dependent. Small increases in the amount taken can lead to significant intensification of the effect. How GHB acts is heavily influenced by body weight, drug interactions, and individual reactions.

These unique attributes of GHB have led to both legitimate and illicit uses. Laborit, the chemist credited for discovering

GHB, mentioned in a scientific publication that GHB possesses possible aphrodisiac properties.[39] In Europe, GHB is used as an anesthetic, as an adjunct medication in childbirth, as a potential pharmacotherapy for the treatment of alcoholism, and for narcolepsy therapy. Only this last use, for treatment

## DATE RAPE DRUG OR ORPHAN DRUG?

Although GHB has obvious uses as a date rape drug, some experts see it as a so-called "orphan drug"—one that is not marketed widely (at least legally) because it does not have enough uses to make it profitable. In fact, one of GHB's only legitimate uses is for the treatment of narcolepsy.

Narcolepsy is a rare disease characterized by excessive daytime sleepiness. It has a prevalence of 0.05% in the general population and affects an estimated 140,000 people in the United States. In 2002, the FDA approved sodium oxybate (Xyrem®) for the treatment of cataplexy in patients with narcolepsy. The active ingredient in this drug is gamma hydroxybutyrate, or GHB. The development and marketing of sodium oxybate was permitted after a revision of the Date Rape Prevention Act of 2000 (see Chapter 5) that allowed GHB to be legally administered for medical purposes.

Because GHB can be abused, carries a risk of possible drug diversion, and presents obvious safety concerns, the FDA set up the Xyrem Risk Management Program. This system is designed to meet the needs of the prescribing physician and the patient while also ensuring the safe distribution of the drug. This is done by registering prescribing physicians, by not stocking the drug in retail pharmacies, and by performing rigorous post-marketing evaluations.

of narcolepsy, is currently approved by the Food and Drug Administration (FDA) in the United States.

## GHB AND CHILDBIRTH

GHB is gaining popularity in France and Italy as an aid in childbirth because it induces remarkable hypotonia, or muscle relaxation.[40] GHB has been reported to cause spectacular action on the dilation of the cervix, decreased anxiety, greater intensity and frequency of uterine contractions, and increased sensitivity to drugs used to induce contractions. It also produces a lack of respiratory depression in the fetus, and protection against fetal cardiac anoxia (lack of oxygen to the heart, especially in cases where the umbilical cord wraps around the fetus's neck).[41]

## GHB AND SLEEP

The effects of GHB on sleep have been well documented. Even small doses produce relaxation, tranquillity, and drowsiness. A sufficiently high dose of GHB will induce sudden sleep within 5 to 10 minutes. Although other sedative-hypnotics interfere with various stages of the sleep cycle and prevent the body from achieving complete and balanced rest, GHB-induced sleep seems to closely resemble normal physiological sleep.[42] In a clinical study, GHB has been shown to induce sleep rapidly without suppressing REM sleep, thereby improving sleep quality.[43]

The main disadvantage of GHB's use as a sleep aid is its short half-life. As soon as GHB's effects wear off (in about 3 hours), people have a tendency to wake up. This pattern, termed "the dawn effect," is more prevalent with higher doses of the drug. Some people take low doses of GHB, while others choose to take a second dose of GHB to help them sleep for another 3 hours. However, not everyone can be put to sleep by GHB. Studies have shown that at doses that make most people fall asleep, some people remain conscious and alert.

## GHB AND ALCOHOLISM

GHB use in the treatment of substance abuse is common in European countries.[44] The drug is used primarily to relieve withdrawal symptoms, cravings, and anxiety among alcoholics. Laboratory rats addicted to alcohol display withdrawal symptoms that closely resemble those exhibited by humans, including tremors and convulsions. Sufficiently high doses of GHB administered to the rats blocked all of these withdrawal symptoms (including anxiety, restlessness, insomnia, tremors, and intermittent tachycardia).[45]

A multicenter clinical study was conducted with GHB in the treatment of 179 patients who were experiencing alcohol withdrawal symptoms.[46] Serious side effects remained low to moderate during the study and the drug was well tolerated. During the study period, 78% of the treated patients attained complete abstinence. Thirty patients remained abstinent one year later. The only side effect reported was occasional and transient dizziness. Researchers have surmised that GHB may be effective in the suppression of withdrawal symptoms in alcoholics.

## GHB AND NARCOLEPSY

In June 2001, a government advisory panel convened by the FDA concluded that GHB could be useful as a treatment for cataplexy, a rare but dangerous complication of the sleep disorder narcolepsy. This panel was asked to consider whether prescription sales should be permitted for GHB under the brand name Xyrem®. The committee concluded that the manufacturer of the drug (Orphan Medical) had shown that Xyrem is useful in treating cataplexy, a complication that can cause people to collapse suddenly when their muscles lose strength.

Orphan Medical received an FDA approval letter in July 2001. The advisory panel urged that if the FDA approved the drug, it should develop a strong risk management plan to ensure that the drug would not fall into the wrong hands. The FDA also requested additional safety data on Xyrem. The subsequent launch of Xyrem as an approved drug came in the fall of 2002.

## GHB OVERDOSE

Overdose with GHB is a real danger. Because GHB generally comes in liquid form, and because the concentration of this liquid is difficult to determine, it is relatively common for people to accidentally take a larger dose of GHB than intended. A dose of only about twice the amount that produces a relaxing effect can cause unpleasant and possibly dangerous side effects. At the overdose level, individuals may experience extreme grogginess (including nodding in and out of consciousness) or unconsciousness, extreme dizziness and disorientation, and vomiting. With higher overdoses (or poisonings), users may become unconscious, and may have convulsions, bradycardia (slow heart rate), vomiting, and depressed breathing. Unconsciousness and vomiting are an extremely dangerous combination. Vomiting while unconscious can lead to aspiration (breathing in) of the vomit, which can cause damage to the lungs and ultimately suffocation and death.

GHB overdose is usually characterized by a strong drowsy feeling followed by a temporarily unrousable sleep (sometimes characterized as a type of coma or a "blackout") for one to four hours. During this "blackout" period, the user or victim is physically incapacitated or helpless, and is unable to consent to or reject sexual advances. Victims of GHB-facilitated rape may not seek help until days after a date rape incident, if at all, in part because the drug impairs memory, causing anterograde amnesia.

## ADDICTION

GHB has been a popular drug of abuse for about a decade, and information is beginning to emerge that it is possible for users

to become addicted to GHB. Addiction is defined as a chronic neurobiological disease in which the user experiences uncontrollable, compulsive drug seeking and use even in the face of negative health and social consequences.[47] Although many users do not consider GHB addiction as dangerous as addiction to, for example, cocaine or heroin, there are reports of users who have problems regulating GHB usage and experience physical withdrawal symptoms after periods of heavy use. The problems in regulating use of GHB seem similar to the habituation and addiction that occur with heavy alcohol use. The main difference between GHB and alcohol use is that people generally feel better after coming down off a single heavy use of GHB than they do with severe alcohol hangovers. This has led to a perception that GHB has fewer negative side effects when used heavily.

Frequent, heavy use of GHB, however, may have some very negative physical and mental side effects. There are reports of serious withdrawal symptoms, including death. Many people find themselves using GHB more often then they intended to do. Using GHB every weekend can turn into using GHB a few times a week or every night. For some people, habitual use can increase to several times a day. People who find themselves using GHB each day or even multiple times a day for periods of weeks or months often report that they have difficulty ceasing use. Some people have also reported that after using GHB daily for many months, they experience strange psychophysical effects, such as constantly hearing bells ringing.

Physical withdrawal symptoms appear in some people who stop using GHB after more than a few consecutive days of repeated use. Symptoms can include difficulty sleeping, anxiety, edginess, chest pain and tightness, muscle and bone aches, sensitivity to external stimuli (sound, light, and touch), depression, and mental dullness. The symptoms last between a few days and 2 to 3 weeks as the body comes back into balance.

Users who take GHB every two to three hours are at increased risk for the emergence of severe withdrawal symptoms, beginning with anxiety, insomnia, tremors, and episodes of abnormally fast heart rate, which may progress rapidly to a state of uncontrolled delirium and agitation. The signs and symptoms of GHB withdrawal appear quickly, generally one to six hours after the last dose, due to the drug's short duration of action and rapid elimination. The course of GHB withdrawal symptoms may be prolonged, persisting for up to two weeks or more. After acute detoxification, many patients report symptoms of anxiety, depression, insomnia, and cognitive deficits that continue for many months.

## TREATMENT

With the increasing popularity of GHB as both a recreational and date rape drug, the number of overdoses seen in emergency rooms in the United States has also been rising. Reports of methods to treat GHB overdoses have been surfacing in scientific and medical literature.

Because of the relative newness and recent popularity of GHB as an abused substance, standard drug or toxicological screening tests do not look for GHB. However, there are analytical tests that can detect GHB levels in blood, urine, or even hair samples after ingestion of the drug. In order to reliably detect GHB in blood or urine samples, testing must be done shortly after the ingestion of GHB, usually within 24 hours. It is unlikely, though, that an individual would be tested for GHB without having a very specific reason to believe that he or she has it in his or her system, such as a possible drink tampering and/or date rape episode.

The management of GHB ingestion depends on the symptoms that the patient displays. Most often, physicians monitor the patient's oxygen status. If the physician suspects that the patient has taken a combination of GHB and another

drug, treatment may include activated charcoal (a black powder that the patient ingests to help absorb poisons or drugs) or gastric lavage (stomach pumping). If a patient is having difficulty breathing, intubation (placing a tube in the airway) is recommended. Several pharmacological agents have been tested as possible antidotes to GHB-induced unconsciousness, the most common of which is physostigmine, a drug that has proven useful in terminating the sedative effects of GHB. In a study of 25 patients anesthetized with GHB who received a low dose of physostigmine (2 milligrams, intravenously), the mean time to awakening was 6.2 minutes. Preliminary reports in unresponsive GHB overdose patients receiving the same dose of physostigmine have produced similar results.[48]

## STATISTICS

GHB-related deaths have occurred in several states. In 1999, there were three reported deaths involving GHB in Texas and two in Minnesota. Missouri has reported five GHB-related deaths and two near-deaths in which GHB was used to facilitate rapes. In Florida, during 2000, GHB was detected in 23 deaths and identified as the cause of death in 6 others. Since 1990, the DEA has documented more than 15,600 overdoses and law enforcement encounters and 72 deaths related to GHB.

Since 2000, GHB has been included in the University of Michigan's Monitoring the Future questionnaire. Survey results indicate that annual GHB use by secondary school students in 2000 ranged from 1.1% among tenth graders to 1.2% among eighth graders and 1.9% among twelfth graders. In 2001, estimates of annual GHB use ranged from 1.0% among tenth graders to 1.1% among eighth graders and 1.6% among twelfth graders.

In 2000, according to the National Drug Intelligence Center (NDIC), GHB availability was either stable or increasing in nearly every DEA field division and High Intensity Drug Trafficking Area. Many areas reported that the increased availability of GHB occurred in concert with a rise in rave activity. Law enforcement also reported increases in the number of cases involving the GHB precursors GBL and 1,4-BD.

The Substance Abuse and Mental Health Service Administration (SAMHSA) reported that emergency room admissions involving GHB nearly quadrupled nationwide from 1998 to 2000, when 4,969 cases were reported (Figure 3.2). Although United States officials do not keep statistics on how many people use particular drugs, survey data indicate that more people are overdosing on GHB than on Ecstasy (MDMA), which is the most popular club drug. In 2000, 2,482 GHB users visited emergency rooms for overdose compared to 1,742 Ecstasy users. Health officials say that these statistics are an indication that GHB is more dangerous than Ecstasy and that the drug is gaining in popularity.

The federal Drug Abuse Warning Network (DAWN) reports that the cities in which GHB is appearing most often are Atlanta, Georgia; Dallas, Texas; Denver, Colorado; New Orleans, Louisiana; and San Francisco, California. Of the GHB users who went to emergency rooms in 1999, 56% said they had used the drug with alcohol, whereas 15% had used it with Ecstasy.

According to *Pulse Check: Trends in Drug Abuse*, GHB users and sellers tend to be middle-class white males between the ages of 18 and 30. GHB is typically packaged in plastic bottles (generally water or sports drink bottles) and distributed by the capful for $5 to $20 per dose. Other popular packaging includes eyedropper bottles, glass vials, and mouthwash bottles.

## LEGISLATION

The FDA banned over-the-counter sales of GHB in 1990, making its use illegal except under strict guidelines and when monitored by a doctor. In February 2000, President Bill Clinton signed federal legislation (H.R. 213) that reclassified

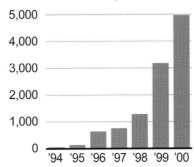

# E.R. visits up from GHB usage

The use of an illegal party drug that is also used as a "date-rape" drug has risen in recent years. GHB, or gamma hydroxybutyrate, is a hallucinogen that causes intoxication and incapacitation.

**Estimated number of visits to U.S. emergency rooms due to GHB/GBL usage***

\* Gamma butyrolactone, or GBL, is a derivative of GHB.

SOURCES: Department of Health and **AP** Human Services; www.projectghb.org

**Figure 3.2** This graph indicates the alarming increase in emergency room visits due to overdoses of GHB. The number of visits resulting from GHB usage more than doubled between 1998 and 2000.

GHB as a Schedule I drug having no medical use. The new law made possession of GHB a felony punishable by up to 20 years in prison. However, in July 2002, a form of GHB was designated as a Schedule III substance, one that is useful for a medical purpose but that cannot be sold, distributed, or provided to anyone for any reason other than its prescribed use. The rescheduling of GHB was done in response to the research showing that GHB can help treat some symptoms of narcolepsy.

## CASE REPORTS
### Case #1

At 2:00 A.M. on a Saturday morning, a 20-year-old male with no previous history of drug or alcohol use was admitted to an emergency room because of cardiac arrest with cardio-pulmonary resuscitation in progress. He was pronounced dead at 2:20 A.M.

On Friday night, he had been at a local dance club, where he was reported to have ingested soft drinks. An autopsy was performed, and multiple toxicological screens of blood and bile samples did not detect alcohol or other drugs. However, eight days later, a test on previously obtained serum detected a level of 27 milligrams/Liter of GHB.

This young man had been poisoned by GHB that was added to his soft drinks without his knowledge. It is worth noting that primary toxicological screens did not identify the presence of GHB. There must be a strong suspicion of GHB use or abuse in order to test for its presence. It is not one of the five drugs—forms of marijuana, cocaine, amphetamines, heroin, and PCP—for which standard drug tests normally screen.

### Case #2

A 17-year-old girl, who was unresponsive after several episodes of vomiting, was taken to an emergency room 2-1/2 hours after ingesting a mixture of GHB and alcohol. She was admitted to the hospital's intensive-care unit. There, the doctors attending to her discovered that she had aspirated (or inhaled) the contents of her stomach into her lung tissue. The young woman experienced generalized seizures before her condition began to improve. Once her lungs cleared, she was placed on supportive care and eventually made a full recovery. Unlike the young man in the first case history, this woman was very lucky to have survived her experience with GHB.

# 4

# Ketamine

Ketamine, more commonly known on the street as "Special K" and to the scientist as ketamine hydrochloride, is a unique drug with a combination of pharmacological effects. Although it is primarily used by veterinarians as an animal tranquilizer, it is available for limited uses in humans. Chemically, it is similar to phencyclidine (PCP or angel dust), a Schedule II drug that was the first of a new class of general anesthetics called dissociative anesthetics. As the name implies, dissociative anesthetics produce in patients a feeling of detachment and disconnection from pain and the environment.

Those who take ketamine report feelings of fragmentation, detachment, and what has been described as psychic/physical/spiritual scatter.[49] Ketamine also has stimulant, depressant, hallucinogenic, amnesic, and analgesic properties. Though it may produce a lack of responsive awareness to the general environment in the user, it does not cause a corresponding depression of autonomic reflexes and vital centers in the brain, making ketamine a powerful date rape drug. In addition to its use in facilitating rape, ketamine is also abused as a "club drug," taken during raves or dance parties.

## HISTORY

In 1958, phencyclidine (PCP) was introduced into clinical anesthesia as an injectable anesthetic agent. PCP had physiological properties that made it a useful anesthetic. The most significant of these was that it was quite effective but had no risk of cardiac or respiratory depression, as was typical of classical general anesthetic agents.

However, due to an unacceptably high incidence of hallucinations, confusion, psychotic reactions, and delirium, it was discontinued for human use in 1963. PCP became commercially available as a veterinary anesthetic in the 1960s under the trade name Sernylan®. In the early 1970s, PCP was classified as a Schedule III compound, and in 1978, it was moved from Schedule III to Schedule II, which classifies it as a drug with a high potential for abuse but with approved medical uses.

In 1962, chemists at Parke-Davis labs who were searching for a replacement for phencyclidine synthesized ketamine hydrochloride. In 1965, scientists learned that ketamine was a useful anesthetic. Marketed under the brand name Ketalar®, it was a promising anesthetic because it suppressed breathing much less than most other available anesthetics did. Ketamine, like PCP, produces minimal cardiac and respiratory effects, and it wears off soon after administration.[50]

In the 1970s, however, the scientific community began to discover some of the negative side effects of ketamine, including visual hallucinations and delirium. Since then, ketamine has become popular with two types of drug users. The first group uses ketamine in a solitary fashion to seek a paranormal experience or to enhance a spiritual journey. Users of this type increased in number after the 1978 publication of the book *The Scientist* by John Lilly. Dr. Lilly's book described using ketamine chronically for a spiritual purpose. Some users report taking the drug, as users of hallucinogens do, to achieve so-called higher forms of consciousness. The second type of ketamine user abuses the drug socially at dance clubs or raves. In the early 1990s, this type of user was publicized by the media and lawmakers, as was the use of ketamine as a date rape drug. This led to the emergency scheduling of ketamine, a previously unscheduled drug, as a Schedule III drug in August 1999 (Figure 4.1).[51]

| Ketamine Terminology | |
|---|---|
| **The Substance** | Ketamine, K, Special K, Ketaset, Ketalar, Vitamin K, Lady K |
| **The Experience** | Tripping, k-ing, the k-hole |

**Figure 4.1** Ketamine has many names, both for the drug itself and for the experience of taking the drug. These are some of the most popular street terms for ketamine and its use.

## PHARMACOLOGY

Ketamine is a compound with a molecular structure similar to that of phencyclidine (Figure 4.2). The pharmaceutical versions of ketamine are clear, colorless liquids available in varying concentrations of 10, 50, and 100 milligram/milliliter solutions (Figure 4.3). Many recreational users inject this liquid intramuscularly or intravenously. It is the liquid formulation that is used as a date rape drug. Liquid ketamine, which is clear and colorless, can easily be slipped into a drink without being detected.

The liquid form of ketamine is sometimes baked to yield a solid form that is often sold on the street as a fine white powder. This powdered form can be snorted, smoked, or packed into gel caps and taken orally. These ketamine pills are usually very diluted and cut with a stimulant such as caffeine or ephedrine (a natural amphetamine-like chemical).

In its powdered form, ketamine is often mistaken for cocaine or crystal methamphetamine. Reports also indicate that ketamine is sometimes sold as Ecstasy (MDMA) and mixed with other drugs. In all its forms, ketamine is usually sold for $25 to $50 per gram.[52]

The dose of abused ketamine varies depending upon the method of administration. If ketamine is snorted, the range of

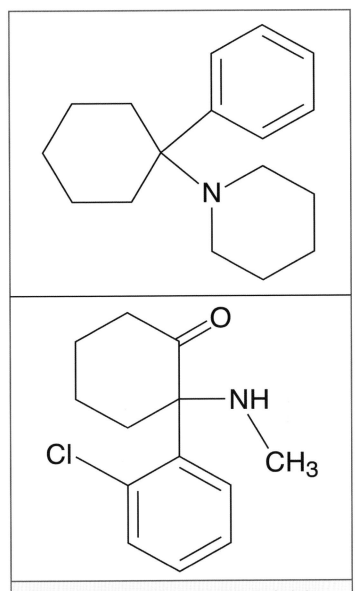

**Figure 4.2** Ketamine (top) was originally synthesized when chemists were attempting to find an alternative to phencyclidine (PCP). PCP (bottom) had previously been used as an anesthetic, but it had a high potential for abuse. The chemical structures of both ketamine and phencyclidine are illustrated here.

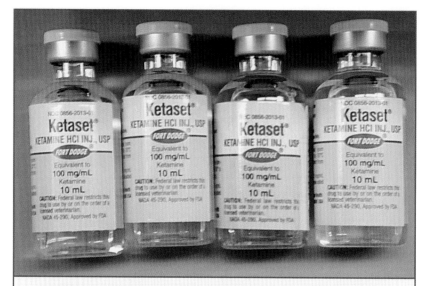

**Figure 4.3** Ketamine is sold for veterinary use in liquid form under the brand name Ketaset ®. Because drug abusers know ketamine is readily available in veterinary clinics, this may put animal health professionals at risk for attack or burglary by people who want to obtain the otherwise illegal drug.

recreational doses varies from 15 to 200 milligrams. If injected intramuscularly, the dose varies from 25 to 125 milligrams. If taken orally, the dose is higher, ranging from 75 to 300 milligrams. Although it is difficult to quantify the dose, ketamine can also be sprinkled on a joint (marijuana cigarette) and smoked. The dose necessary for use as an anesthesia falls at the upper end of the recreational range. The lethal dose is nearly 30 times that of the anesthetic dose. Accordingly, there is minimal risk of overdosing, which is one reason the drug appeals to recreational users.[53]

When ketamine is injected, it takes 5 minutes for the user to begin to feel the effect of the drug. Intranasal users experience the effects within about 10 minutes. The beginning stages of the effects are slight euphoria, tingling sensations, and increased heart rate. Within the first 30 minutes, the principal dissociative effects of the drug occur and then subside gradually. When taken orally, the bulk of the ketamine "trip" will last for approximately 1 to 3 hours.[54] Users have reported feeling light-headed, dizzy, and nauseated for several hours, both during and after taking ketamine. Although the drug's effects can still be felt, users are not incapacitated the following day. Unlike with other forms of general anesthesia, the user's eyes remain open and constantly move or jerk from side to side (a condition termed *nystagmus*).

The duration of the drug's action depends on the method of administration. Upon recovery from ketamine, the patient or user may be agitated, disoriented, restless, and tearful. This is called "emergence delirium." Patients may continue to experience unpleasant dreams up to 24 hours after the drug has been taken. Flashbacks have been reported, and their incidence may be higher than with many hallucinogens.[55]

## MECHANISM OF ACTION

Ketamine exerts its physiological effects at the molecular level by interfering with the actions of excitatory amino acid neurotransmitters, primarily glutamate, the most prevalent excitatory neurotransmitter in the brain. The excitatory neurotransmitters regulate numerous functions of the central nervous system.

### A TEEN'S EXPERIENCE WITH KETAMINE

I snorted a fair amount, probably between 60–150 milligrams. I felt it going down the back of my throat. I feel kind of sick now (12 hours after I used it, and I've been to sleep, of course). Is it normal to feel sick? Basically, it just feels as though my stomach is upset. . . .

The people I was doing the ketamine with told me that it was extremely clean ketamine. It did indeed look clean. However, it burnt like hell when I insufflated it.

Adapted from: DanceSafe E-Board. Available online at
*http://www.dancesafe.org/ubbthreads/postlist.php?Cat=&Board=UBB16.*

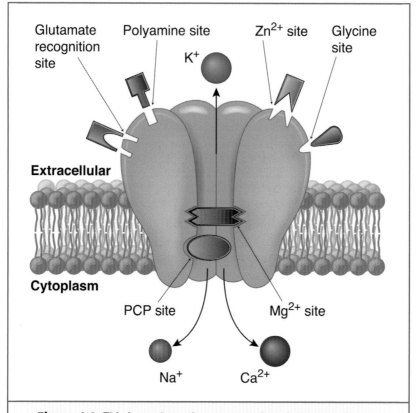

**Figure 4.4** This is a schematic representation of the N-methyl-D-aspartate (NMDA) receptor. Both ketamine and phencyclidine block the flow of ions through this receptor, which causes their effects on the central nervous system.

Ketamine binds to the excitatory amino acid receptor known as the N-methyl-D-aspartate (NMDA) receptor complex, which regulates calcium flow through an ion channel (Figure 4.4). Therefore, ketamine's direct action is to block the movement of calcium through this channel.[56]

Ketamine acts as a noncompetitive antagonist of NMDA receptors. It induces changes of perception, memory, and cognition throughout the brain. Drugs like ketamine are said to work globally, meaning that they directly or indirectly affect several neurotransmitter systems. Nonetheless, the main effects of ketamine appear to result from its actions as an NMDA antagonist.[57]

## PHYSIOLOGICAL EFFECTS

Because ketamine is available for clinical and veterinary use, it has been studied extensively. Recreational users of ketamine report feeling both anesthetized and sedated. The most sought-after effect is the feeling of dissociation, where the user has a distorted perception of the body, environment, and time. Users refer to this sensation as an "out-of-body experience." The dissociation of one's own consciousness and the near-death feeling is also referred to by the slang term "K-hole."

Studies have shown that ketamine substantially disrupts both attention and learning.[58] Research volunteers using the drug fail to modify their behavior in response to feedback. They take longer to learn new tasks and do not apply strategy. Ketamine was also shown to cause changes in perception, impairments in tests of vigilance and verbal fluency, and to produce behaviors similar to those seen in schizophrenia. Someone who has recently taken ketamine may exhibit catatonia—a tendency to remain in a fixed, stuporous state, with a flat face, open mouth, dilated pupils, "sightless staring," and rigid posturing. At higher dosages, the user enters a state characterized by motor impairment, social withdrawal, autistic behavior, an inability to maintain a cognitive set, poor and idiosyncratic thought patterns, and bizarre responses.

People who use ketamine regularly can suffer psychological problems. Paranoia and delirium are the main difficulties.[59] There are many reports of regular ketamine users starting to see patterns and coincidences (synchronicities) in the world around them. To users, these patterns indicate that they are somehow more important or integral to the world than other people, and this can also contribute to their feelings of paranoia.

Other psychological problems also occur with ketamine abuse. Research and anecdotal reports have shown that it is possible that use of ketamine can induce the feeling of a near-death experience. The typical feature of a "classic" near-death experience is the perception of separating from the body (out-of-body experiences). Most near-death experiences have happened to users who take ketamine intravenously or intramuscularly. Most users were not trying to have the experience through autosuggestion or a hypnotic trance.[60] Many users have seemed frightened and/or confused by what happened—even to the extent of doubting their own sanity. In the clinical setting, patients can be prevented from having near-death experiences by giving them benzodiazepine sedatives along with ketamine, which can produce true unconsciousness rather than dissociation.

If an overdose of ketamine is suspected, it is possible to test for the presence of the drug in urine, blood, and hair samples. However, both standard and extended drug tests do not routinely test for ketamine. Unless there is a particular reason to be looking for it, medical personnel do not request specific ketamine tests. It is not one of the five drugs (marijuana, opioids, cocaine, amphetamines, and PCP) that are included in standard and extended drug tests. If testing for ketamine is requested, the breakdown product of ketamine, called norketamine, is detectable in both blood and urine for 7 to 14 days after a single administration. Because of their similarities in chemical structure, ketamine may cause false positives for PCP on some drug screens. However, more sensitive follow-up testing can clearly distinguish between the two drugs. This was a more significant issue before 1999, when ketamine was not an illegal substance.[61]

## CLINICAL USE

Ketamine has unique properties that make it useful for certain pediatric procedures and for anesthetizing patients who are at risk for hypotension (low blood pressure) or bronchospasm (overly responsive airways). However, significant side effects limit its routine use. Ketamine rapidly produces a state of hypnosis distinctly different from that of other anesthetics. Patients display profound analgesia (absence of a sense of pain without a loss of consciousness), are unresponsive to commands, and exhibit amnesia, yet usually keep their eyes open throughout the experience. Patients may also move their limbs involuntarily and usually maintain spontaneous breathing.

Ketamine is generally administered to patients intravenously, but it is also effective when administered by intramuscular, oral, and rectal routes. The onset of action is generally short (10 to 15 minutes) but the duration of anesthesia of a single dose is long. Ketamine is the only intravenous anesthetic that produces an increase in heart rate and arterial blood pressure. It can also markedly increase cerebral blood flow, oxygen consumption, and intracranial pressure.

Although ketamine is a desirable anesthetic in many respects, its dissociative effects (disorientation, sensory and perceptual illusions, and hallucinations) and the possibility of "emergence delirium" (hallucinations and unpleasant dreams that occur when ketamine is wearing off) have limited its use in general surgery. It is considered useful for certain geriatric patients and patients in shock because of its cardiostimulatory properties; for patients with asthma; and for children undergoing short, painful procedures, such as treatment of burns.

## ADDICTION AND TREATMENT

Death due to the use or misuse of ketamine is rare. Only severe overdoses present substantial risk, and such incidents are usually treated in the intensive-care unit. The most dangerous effects of ketamine are behavioral. Individuals may become withdrawn, paranoid, and very uncoordinated. Physicians can only treat overdoses of this type symptomatically, by offering calm reassurance and an environment with little stimulation.

Physicians can also treat overdose symptoms with benzodi-azepines to control the anxiety associated with ketamine.

Ketamine can be psychologically addictive. Individuals who use it regularly may find it difficult to stop. These users experience drug craving and develop a high tolerance but show no evidence of physiological withdrawal syndrome.[62] Ketamine can be called a "reinforcing drug," which means that taking the drug can be pleasurable. Numerous reports exist of individuals who became dependent on ketamine and use it daily. Addiction to ketamine has a strong psychological component. What a person experiences with ketamine use is a feeling of dissociation accompanied by extreme euphoria. These episodes can become very psychologically addicting.

Unlike opiates, such as heroin, which have a stronger component of physical addiction, ketamine is more strongly psychologically addictive. The first step in the treatment of ketamine addiction is the detoxification stage, in which the drug is cleaned out of the body. This is something that should be closely supervised by a physician or other health-care professional to prevent the user from abusing the drug when cravings set in. After detoxification, the next step is to have the user seek group therapy and counseling to adjust to life without the drug.

## STATISTICS

Since 1992, the DEA has received more than 500 reports of the sale and/or use of ketamine by minors on college campuses, at nightclubs, and at raves.[63] Most DEA field divisions report that ketamine is available in their areas, while several indicate that availability is increasing.[64] The sale of ketamine as a drug of abuse to undercover law enforcement officials has also been recorded. The DEA's STRIDE data have shown that since 1999 (the first year that ketamine was included in the STRIDE data system), there has been an upward trend in ketamine seizures. In 1999, 4,551 dosage units of ketamine were seized, compared with only 3,185 dosage units in 2000. In 2001, a large increase in the confiscation of ketamine was reported, with 111,478 dosage units seized, which is a 35-fold increase in only two years.

The Monitoring the Future (MTF) survey is an indicator of the consequences of ketamine use. It, too, shows general upward trends. MTF data indicate that between 2001 and 2002, use of ketamine held steady for eighth graders at 1.3% and rose (although not significantly) for tenth (2.1% to 2.2%) and twelfth graders (2.5% to 2.6%). In addition, the Drug Abuse Warning Network (DAWN) also reports an increase in the consequences of ketamine use, including the number of ketamine-related hospital emergency room episodes. According to DAWN, emergency room mentions of ketamine use increased almost 36-fold over seven years, from a low of 19 reported cases in 1994 to 679 in 2001.[65]

## TRAFFICKING

Ketamine became a controlled Schedule III substance in August 1999 based on DEA data documenting the growing abuse of this drug. The marketed forms of ketamine—Ketalar (for human use) and Ketaset, Ketajet, and Vetalar® (for veterinary use)—are available only to licensed medical and veterinary personnel. Clandestine manufacture of ketamine has not been encountered because, in contrast to that of PCP, the synthesis of ketamine is a complex and time-consuming process. For this reason, the vast majority of ketamine distributed in the United States is diverted or stolen from legitimate sources, particularly veterinary clinics.

By placing ketamine into Schedule III, the DEA is saying, based on medical and scientific evaluations, that:

1. Ketamine has a lower potential for abuse than the drugs or other substances in Schedules I and II.

2. Ketamine currently has accepted medical use in the United States.

3. Abuse of ketamine may lead to low or moderate physical dependence or high psychological dependence.

## CASE REPORTS
### Case #1

On a Saturday morning, a 28-year-old woman was found unconscious in her bedroom by her roommate. Police were "highly suspicious" that the woman was drugged at some point the evening before. Officers found the woman without any clothing on and tests showed evidence of sexual assault.

Officers added, however, that they also suspected drug involvement because, according to the woman, the amount of alcohol she had ingested would not have caused her condition. "She couldn't recall how she got to where she was found," said an officer. The women's roommate said, "She was wrapped up in my blanket and I could see that she wasn't wearing any clothes." The roommate also added that the woman's clothes were not in her room when she called the police.

Upon waking, the woman reported that she had been at a friend's party earlier in the evening, where she had been drinking beer. She said she had also been to a dance club in town later in the evening. She said she spent the latter part of the evening with a group of men at the club, where she consumed about five beers. Also at the club, the woman and one male acquaintance had snorted what the woman had thought were several lines of cocaine.

The roommate who found the unconscious woman said that three officers responded to her call, and that a female officer succeeded in waking the woman. "At first, she couldn't speak coherently," the roommate said. "I've never heard anyone talking like that. There was something in her system. She didn't seem hungover or drunk."

Certain drugs can cause this blackout effect, including ketamine, which is available in a white powder form that resembles cocaine. However, instead of the stimulant effects of cocaine, ketamine causes a dissociative state, sedation, and anesthesia. Although the woman assumed she was snorting cocaine, it appears that she was misled into taking a very different drug from what she intended to consume.

The investigation in the case is still open, and police have not ruled out the possibility that a drug played a role in incapacitating the woman. No criminal action has been taken at this point.

## Case #2

Dr. Nicholas Willert's small, suburban animal clinic was robbed in April. His wife, Mary Willert, who works at the clinic, said two men came in one afternoon and requested treatment for their toy poodle. After the dog was examined, one of the men drew a gun and demanded all the ketamine in the clinic. Mrs. Willert directed them to a cabinet containing 17 bottles of the drug.

The men bound the Willerts to chairs with duct tape and also taped their mouths. Before they fled out a back door with the ketamine, one of the men told them, "We didn't harm you, we didn't hurt you. Please forgive us." Mrs. Willert managed to free herself and call the police. Police arrested three men for the robbery, one of whom allegedly drove the getaway vehicle. Police suspect the men were responsible for other ketamine robberies of veterinary clinics as well.

Veterinary clinics can be easy targets for criminals looking for drugs. Because ketamine is not easily synthesized in clandestine laboratories, it must be diverted or stolen from another source.

# 5

# Legal Considerations Associated With Abuse of Date Rape Drugs

**In addition to putting yourself** in serious physical danger by using the drugs Rohypnol, GHB, and ketamine, you are exposing yourself to possible criminal liability when you do so. This chapter discusses the criminal laws that apply to the abuse of date rape drugs—laws that punish those who use these date rape drugs recreationally and those who use them to commit crimes against others.

## CRIMINALIZING THE ABUSE OF DATE RAPE DRUGS

Several states and the federal government have passed laws explicitly banning the recreational use of club drugs. In particular, at least 20 states and the federal government have made it illegal to manufacture, use, possess, or distribute date rape drugs. In addition, even in those states that have not passed statutes specifically addressing date rape drugs, law enforcement officials have utilized the state's general drug statutes to punish offenders for committing crimes involving these types of illicit drugs.

Various factors, such as the amount of drugs involved in the crime and the type of criminal activity involved (for example, possession for recreational use versus distribution), determine the penalties associated with the violations of these laws. Punishment can range anywhere from 1 year in prison to life imprisonment. Based on the tough sentencing laws that have emerged in the United States, it is clear that state and federal law enforcement officials are aware of the increased interest in, and use of, date rape drugs among teenagers and adults, and are responding by treating date rape drugs as some of the most serious controlled substances.

In addition to prosecuting criminals who use, possess, distribute, and manufacture date rape drugs, every state and the federal government has made it a crime to use date rape drugs in connection with a crime of physical violence, such as rape. Some state sexual assault or rape statutes take drugging into account in terms of grading the severity of the sexual offense, while others use it as a factor in determining the length of the sentence given to the perpetrator. Nonconsensual sexual conduct with incapacitated individuals—whether facilitated by alcohol or other types of incapacitating drugs—has been a societal problem dating back to the time that rape convictions were first recorded in the United States. As early as the first part of the 19th century, perpetrators were prosecuted and convicted for sexually assaulting persons who were intoxicated with alcohol. Although the most common scenario involved a victim who voluntarily ingested alcohol and then was unable to fight off the attacker's advances, in a few reported cases, the victim was forced to ingest alcohol and was subsequently raped. Early on, many defendants attempted to draw a distinction between involuntary and voluntary ingestion and criminal responsibility for rape. However, courts rejected such a distinction, because, in either case, the victim's intoxicated state rendered the victim unable to consent to the sexual contact.

There have been a number of cases involving rapes facilitated by drugs other than the date rape drugs Rohypnol, GHB, and ketamine. In these cases, the defendants used drugs that were readily available, including codeine, cocaine, glue, sleeping pills, antihistamines, opiates, benzodiazepines (tranquilizers), amphetamines, barbiturates, and antidepressants. As with the cases involving alcohol consumption, some of the victims voluntarily ingested the drug, while others did so unwittingly. Again, in either situation, rape laws treat the perpetrator the same, regardless of how the victim became incapacitated.

Armed with the wealth of knowledge and experience gained from prosecuting rape cases involving the use of drugs and/or alcohol, law enforcement officials have stepped up their efforts to prevent and prosecute date rape drug cases, stiffening penalties and increasing efforts to encourage victims to come forward and report sexual assaults. Despite the best efforts of federal, state, and local law enforcement, the incidence of drug-induced sexual assaults continues to rise, especially in the teen and college-age population.

One reason for the continued rise in drug-facilitated sexual assault stems from the unique characteristics of date rape drugs themselves—characteristics that distinguish them from alcohol and other types of drugs used in the past. For example, the drugs Rohypnol and GHB result in a loss of consciousness and memory, and the effects are augmented with the use of alcohol. Victims often do not remember the attack itself; they wake up knowing only that something wrong has occurred. Unlike alcohol and other types of drugs, these drugs render victims completely incapacitated. Because it sometimes takes days for a victim to piece together enough information to realize that he or she has been sexually assaulted while unconscious, the reporting of the incident is delayed. This, in turn, ensures that the physical evidence of rape and the residue of the date rape drug will be long gone from the victim's body. GHB remains in the urine for approximately 12 hours, thus placing a victim who makes a delayed report of rape at a significant disadvantage. Similarly, Rohypnol remains in the urine for only about 48 to 96 hours, providing just a slightly longer window for testing.

Adding to these problems is the reality that Rohypnol, GHB, and ketamine are difficult for victims to detect, which provides the attacker with a distinct advantage. Although it has a somewhat salty taste, when added to a drink, GHB is basically undetectable. When added to carbonated beverages, Rohypnol causes additional fizzing beyond what would be considered normal, but it is still not readily evident to victims because it does not dramatically alter the color or taste of the drink. (It is of note that a reformulation of Rohypnol includes a dye that changes the color of a drink, as discussed in Chapter 2.) Ketamine's availability as a liquid in its veterinary anesthetic preparations makes it easy to slip into drinks and be used as a date rape drug. As a liquid, ketamine is clear and colorless and would be very difficult to detect by sight or taste.

Thus, in sexual assault cases involving date rape drugs, law enforcement officials often are faced with a situation in which the victim has little memory of what has occurred, there is little or no physical evidence of sexual assault or drugging, and the victim does not remember anything unusual about the drink he or she ingested or the person to whom he or she was speaking. Aside from presenting serious proof problems if the rape case goes to trial, these realities often cause victims to refrain from reporting the rape altogether, out of a belief that nothing will be done. Of course, this is not the case. The increased prevalence of cases and experiences involving date rape drugs has made society more aware of the problem and more willing to believe people who have been the victims of drug-facilitated sexual assaults.

## LEGISLATION

The methods criminals use to traffic and distribute illegal drugs are constantly evolving, as are the methods that law enforcement agencies use to combat them. Yet even changes in law enforcement tactics are sometimes not enough to fight the newest drug threats, and federal, state, and local governments must pass new laws to provide these agencies with the tools they need to meet them.

In 1970, Congress passed the Controlled Substances Act (CSA), which allows the DEA, the Department of Health and Human Services, or any interested party to initiate proceedings to add, delete, or change the schedule of a drug. Drugs controlled by the CSA are listed in Schedules I to V. As noted previously, drugs in Schedule I are considered the most dangerous, have the greatest potential for abuse, and have no currently accepted use within the medical profession. Schedule V drugs are the least dangerous, have the lowest potential for abuse, and are accepted in medical treatment of patients. The DEA uses a very rigorous process to place drugs on these schedules.

Congress recognized the growing use of predatory drugs to facilitate sexual assaults when it passed the Drug-Induced Rape Prevention and Punishment Act in 1996. This law established strict federal penalties of imprisonment and fines for anyone convicted of committing a crime of violence, including rape, by administering a controlled substance without the victim's knowledge or consent. Furthermore, in February 2000, Congress passed the Hillory J. Farias and Samantha Reid Date-Rape Drug Prohibition Act of 2000, named for two young women who died after they unwittingly ingested GHB. Among other things, this law makes GHB a Schedule I drug under the CSA.

## The Drug-Induced Rape Prevention and Punishment Act of 1996

The Drug-Induced Rape Prevention and Punishment Act of 1996 provides criminal penalties of up to 20 years imprisonment for any person who distributes a controlled substance, such as Rohypnol, to another person with the intent to commit a violent crime. The act does not criminalize any new conduct in that the distribution of a controlled substance is already a federal crime. It does, however, establish the basis for harsher penalties under federal law if the distribution facilitates a violent crime.

Additional penalties are also imposed with specific reference to Rohypnol. These penalties include the possibility of imprisonment up to 20 years for individuals who knowingly or intentionally manufacture, distribute, or dispense 1 gram of flunitrazepam or up to 5 years for 30 milligrams. The penalties are higher if the person has a prior conviction or if death or serious bodily injury results from the use of the substance.

The Controlled Substance Act provisions relating to import or export are also amended, so that penalties for violations involving Rohypnol are equivalent to penalties for Schedule I drugs. A new penalty of up to three years' imprisonment, or a fine, or both, is added for simple possession of Rohypnol. A new program is established to provide police departments with educational materials on the use of controlled substances during rapes and sexual assaults.

## The Hillory J. Farias and Samantha Reid Date-Rape Drug Prohibition Act of 2000

This legislation places GHB in Schedule I of the CSA. Making GHB a Schedule I drug appropriately reflects Congress's judgment that possession and distribution of GHB should be prohibited and violators subject to stringent criminal sanctions. Until this act was signed, laws regarding GHB were limited primarily to the state level. Enforcement had been slow. This law made GHB a Schedule I drug, while still allowing supervised medical use of GHB for narcolepsy. When the FDA approved GHB for medical use, the act permitted the substance to go back to Schedule III for this limited purpose, while remaining a Schedule I drug for determining the consequences of illicit use. The act also designated ketamine as a Schedule III compound.

The act directs the secretary of the Department of Health and Human Services to develop and implement a plan for a national campaign to educate young adults, youths, law enforcement personnel, teachers, school nurses, rape victim counselors, and hospital emergency room personnel about: (1) the dangers of these drugs, (2) the applicability of the CSA to such drugs, including penalties, (3) how to recognize signs that an individual may be a victim of such drugs, and (4) the appropriate response when an individual exhibits such symptoms. The act also requires the Department of Health and Human Services to collect data on the incidence of drug abuse of this type and report the information annually to Congress.

## CONCLUSION

The implementation of strict laws to punish individuals who commit drug-induced sexual assaults indicates that this

## FICTIONAL CASE APPLYING THE HILLORY J. FARIAS AND SAMANTHA REID DATE-RAPE DRUG PROHIBITION ACT OF 2000

In the 2001 case of *DeVita* v. *Tammaro*, testimony showed that John DeVita, a neurologist, had persuaded Jane Tammaro, who was a nurse, to accompany him on a trip to a medical convention in California. Tammaro told DeVita that she had a boyfriend and was not interested in a sexual relationship with him; she also told him "that if he expected to have a physical relationship with her while on the trip, she would have to cancel her plans to go." Police later found Tammaro dead in a hotel room after receiving a 911 call from DeVita. An autopsy revealed that Tammaro had been sexually assaulted. Toxicology tests demonstrated that she had died from an overdose of GHB.

DeVita was convicted of first-degree murder, rape through the use of drugs, and administering a drug to commit a felony; he was sentenced to life in prison without the possibility of parole.

type of predatory behavior is becoming a growing concern in our society today. The three date rape drugs identified in this book are powerful pharmacological entities, all of them capable of rendering a victim helpless against a sexual assault. Education and awareness as to the science behind date rape drugs can make a difference in preventing the occurrence of this type of attack.

# References

1. Curtis, D. G. "Perspectives on Acquaintance Rape." *The American Academy of Experts in Traumatic Stress, Inc.* 1997. Available online at *http://www.aaets.org/arts/art13.htm.*

2. Fisher, B. S., F. T. Cullen, and M. G. Turner. "Sexual Victimization of College Women: Findings from Tow National-Level Studies." Washington, D.C.: National Institute of Justice and Bureau of Justice Statistics, 2000.

3. Koss, M. P. "Hidden Rape: Sexual Aggression and Victimization in the National Sample of Students in Higher Education." *Violence in Dating Relationships: Emerging Social Issues,* eds. M. A. Pirog-Good and J. E. Stets. New York: Praeger, 1988, pp. 145–168.

4. Koss, 1998.

5. Fisher, 2000.

6. Berkowitz, A. "College Men as Perpetrators of Acquaintance Rape and Sexual Assault: A Review of Recent Research." *Journal of American College Health* 40 (1992): 175–181.

7. Muehlenhard, C. L. "Misinterpreted Dating Behaviors and the Risk of Date Rape." *Violence in Dating Relationships: Emerging Social Issues,* eds. M. A. Pirog-Good and J. E. Stets. New York: Praeger, 1988, pp. 241–256.

8. Berkowitz, 1992.

9. Quackenbush, R. L. "Attitudes of College Men toward Women and Rape." *Journal of College Student Development* 32 (4) (1991): 376–377.

10. Malamuth, N.M. "A Multidimensional Approach to Sexual Aggression: Combining Measures of Past Behavior and Present Likelihood." *Annals of the New York Academy of Sciences* 528 (1998): 123–132.

11. Hall, G.C.N., and R. Hirschman. "Sexual Aggression against Children: a Conceptual Perspective of Etiology." *Criminal Justice and Behavior* 19 (1992): 8–23.

12. Sanday, P. R. *Fraternity Gang Rape: Sex, Brotherhood, and Privilege on Campus.* New York: University Press, 1990; O'Sullivan, C. S. "Acquaintance Gang Rape on Campus." *Acquaintance Rape: The Hidden Crime,* eds. A. Parrot and L. Bechhofer. New York: Wiley, 1991, Chapter 10.

13. Fisher, 2000.

14. Abbey, A., L. Thomson Ross, D. McDuggie, and P. McAuslan. "Alcohol and Dating Risk Factors for Sexual Assault among College Women." *Psychology of Women Quarterly* 20 (1996): 147–169.

15. Koss, 1998.

16. Abbey, A. "Acquaintance Rape and Alcohol Consumption on College Campuses: How Are They Linked?" *College Health* 39 (1991): 165–169.

17. Norris, J., P. Nurius, and T. Graham. "When a Date Changes from Fun to Dangerous." *Violence Against Women* 5 (3) (1999): 230–250.

18. Abbey, 1991.

19. Staten, C. "'Roofies,' the New 'Date Rape' Drug of Choice." *Emergency Net News.* 1996. Available online at *http://www.emergency.com/roofies.htm.*

20. Office of National Drug Control Policy Fact Sheet, 1998.

21. Office of National Drug Control Policy Fact Sheet, February 2003.

22. Negrusz, A., et. al. "Highly Sensitive Micro-Plate Enzyme Immunoassay Screening and NCI-GC-MS Confirmation of Flunitrazepam and Its Major Metabolite 7-Aminoflunitrazepam in Hair." *Journal of Analytical Toxicology* 23 (6) (1999): 429–435.

23. Office of National Drug Control Policy 2002; National Drug Intelligence Center 2003.

24. National Institute of Drug Absue, Monitoring the Future 2002.

25. National Drug Threat Assessment Survey 2003.

26. United States Drug Enforcement Administration Congressional Testimony, July 16, 1996.

27. United States Drug Enforcement Administration Congressional Testimony, March 11, 1999.

28. Li, J., S. A. Stokes, and A. Woeckener. "A Tale of Novel Intoxication: Seven Cases of Gamma-hydroxybutyric Acid Overdose." *Annals of Emergency Medicine* 31 (1998): 723–728

29. Vickers, M. D. "Gamma-hydroxybutyric Acid." *International Anesthesiology Clinics* 71 (1969): 75–89.

30. Caruso, R., M. Ishikawa-Yamaki, and T. Schellenberg. *CEH Product Review*: 1,4-Butanediol. Chemical Economics Handbook, SRI International, 1997.

31. Vree, T. B., J. Damsma, A. G. Van den Bogert, and E. van Der Kleijn. "Pharmacokinetics of 4-hydroxybutyric Acid in Man, Rhesus Monkey and Dog." *Anaesthesiologische und Intensivmedizinische Praxis* 110 (1978): 21–39.

32. Palatini, R., L. Tedeschi, G. Frison, R. Padrini, R. Zordan, R. Orlando, L. Gallimberti, G. L. Gessa, and S. D. Ferrara. "Dose-dependent Absorption and Elimination of Gamma-hydroxybutyric Acid in Healthy Volunteers." *European Journal of Clinical Pharmacology* 45 (1993): 353–356; Tellier, P. P. "Club Drugs: Is It All Ecstasy?" *Pediatric Annals* 31 (9) (2002): 550–556.

33. Drakontides, A. B., J. A. Schneider, and W. H. Funderburk. "Some Effects of Sodium Gamma-hydroxybutyrate on the Central Nervous System." *Journal of Pharmacology and Experimental Therapeutics* 135 (1962): 275–284; Tunnicliff, G. "Significance of Gamma-hydroxybutyric Acid in the Brain." *General Pharmacology* 23 (1992): 1027–1034.

34. Walters J. R., R. H. Roth, and G. K. Aghajanian. "Dopaminergic Neurons: Similar Biochemical and Histochemical Effects of Gamma-hydroxybutyrate and Acute Lesions of the Nigro-neostriatal Pathway." *Journal of Pharmacology and Experimental Therapeutics* 186 (1973): 630–639; Tunnicliff, G. "Sites of Actin of Gamma-hydroxybutyrate (GHB)—A Neuroactive Drug with Abuse Potential." *Journal of Toxicology and Clinical Toxicology* 35 (1997): 581–590.

35. Hechler, V., S. Goebaille, and M. Maitre. "Selective Distribution Pattern of Gamma-hydroxybutyrate Receptors in the Rat Forebrain and Mid-brain as Revealed by Quantitative Autoradiograph." *Brain Research* 572 (1992): 345–348.

# References

36. Takahara, J., S. Yunoki, W. Yakushiji, J. Yamauchi, J. Yamane, and T. Ofuji. "Stimulatory Effects of Gamma-hydroxybutyric Acid on Growth Hormone and Prolactin Release in Humans." *Journal of Clinical Endocrinology and Metabolism* 44 (1977): 1014.

37. McDowell, D. M. "MDMA, Ketamine, GHB, and the 'Club Drug' Scene." *American Psychiatric Press Textbook of Substance Abuse Treatment*, eds. M. Galanter and H. D. Kleber. Washington, D.C.: American Psychiatric Press, 1999; Morgenthaler, J., and D. Joy. "GHB (gamma-hydroxybutyrate)." *Smart Drug News* 3 (6) (1994): 1–41.

38. Vickers, 1996.

39. Laborit, H. "Correlations between Protein and Serotonin Synthesis during Various Activities of the Central Nervous System (slow and desynchronized sleep, learning and memory, sexual activity, morphine tolerance, aggressiveness, and pharmacological action of sodium gamma-hydroxybutyrate)." *Research Communications in Chemical Pathology and Pharmacology* 3 (1) (1972): 58–81.

40. Morgenthaler and Joy, 1994; Vickers, 1969.

41. Laborit, 1964; Vickers, 1969.

42. Entholzner, E., I. Mielke, R. Pichlmeier, F. Weber, and H. Seneck. "EEG Changes During Sedation with Gamma-hydroxybutyric Acid." *Anesthesiology* 44 (5) (1995): 345–350.

43. Mamelak, M. "Neurodegeneration, Sleep, and Cerebral Energy Metabolism: A Testable Hypothesis." *Journal of Geriatric Psychiatry and Neurology* 10 (1) (1997): 29–32.

44. Gallimberti, L., G. Canton, N. Gentile, M. Ferri, M. Cibin, S. D. Ferrara, F. Fadda, and G. L. Gessa. "Gamma-hydroxybutyric Acid for Treatment of Alcohol Withdrawal Syndrome." *Lancet* 2 (8666) (1989): 787–789; Beghe, F., and M. T. Carpanini. "Safety and Tolerability of Gamma-hydroxybutyric Acid in the Treatment of Alcohol-dependant Patients." *Alcohol* 20 (3) (2000): 223–225.

45. Miotto, K., J. Darakjian, J. Basch, S. Murray, J. Zogg, and R. Rawson. "Gamma-hydroxybutyric Acid: Patterns of Use, Effects and Withdrawal." *American Journal of Addiction* 10 (3) (2001): 232–241.

46. Addolorato, G., E. Castelli, G.F. Stefanini, G. Casella, F. Caputo, L. Marsigli, M. Bernardi, and G. Gasbarrini. "An Open Multicentric Study Evaluating 4-hydroxybutyric Acid Sodium Salt in the Medium-term Treatment of 179 Alcohol Dependent Subjects. GHB Study Group." *Alcohol and Alcoholism* 31 (4) (1996): 341–345.

47. Leshner, A. I. "The Essence of Drug Addiction." NIDA Publication. Available online at *http://www.drugabuse.gov/Published_Articles/Essence.html*.

48. Caldicott, D.G., and M. Kuhn. "Gamma-hydroxybutyrate Overdose and Physostigmine: Teaching New Tricks to an Old Drug?" *Annals of Emergency Medicine* 37 (1) (2001): 99–102.

49. McDowell, 1999.

50. Moretti, R. J., S. Z. Hassan, L. I. Goodman, and H. Y. Meltzer. "Comparison of Ketamine and Thiopental in Healthy Volunteers: Effects on Mental Status, Mood, and Personality." *Anesthesia and Analgesia* 63 (12) (1984): 1087–1096.

51. McDowell, 1999.

52. DEA Drug Intelligence Brief, 2000.

53. McDowell, 1999.

54. Delgarno, P. J., and D. Shewan. "Illicit Use of Ketamine in Scotland." *Journal of Psychoactive Drugs* 28 (1996): 191–199.

55. Siegel, R. K. "The Natural History of Hallucinogens." *Hallucinogens: Neurochemistry, Behavioral and Clinical Perspectives.* New York: Raven, 1984, pp. 1–18.

56. Hampton, R. Y., F. Medzihradsky, J. H. Woods, and P. J. Dahlstrom. "Stereospecific Binding of $^3$H Phencyclidine in Brain Membranes." *Life Sciences* 30 (25) (1982): 2147–2154.

57. McDowell, 1999.

58. Krystal, J. H., L. P. Karper, J. P. Seibyl, G. K. Freeman, R. Delaney, J. D. Bremner, G. R. Heninger, M. B. Bowers, Jr., and D. S. Charney. "Subanesthetic Effects of the Noncompetitive NMDA Antagonist Ketamine in Humans." *Archives of General Psychiatry* 51 (3) (1994): 199–214.

59. Malhotra, A. K., D. A. Pinals, H. Weingartner, K. Sirocco, C. D. Missar, D. Pickar, and A. Breier. "NMDA Receptor Function and Human Cognition: the Effects of Ketamine in Healthy Volunteers." *Neuropsychopharmacology* 14 (5) (1996): 301–307.

60. Lilly, J. C. *The Scientist: A Metaphysical Autobiography.* Berkeley, CA: Ronin Publishing Inc., 1997.

61. Simpson, D., R. A. Braithwaite, D. R. Jarvie, M. J. Stewart, S. Walker, I. W. Watson, and B. Widdop. "Screening for Drugs of Abuse (II): Cannabinoids, Lysergic Acid Diethylamide, Buprenorphine, Methadone, Barbiturates, Benzodiazepines and Other Drugs." *Annals of Clinical Biochemistry* 34 (5) (1997): 460–510; Shannon, M. "Toxicology Reviews: Physostigmine." *Pediatric Emergency Care* 14 (3) (1998): 224–226.

62. Jansen, K. L., and R. Darracot-Cankovic. "The Nonmedical Use of Ketamine, Part Two: A Review of Problem Use and Dependence." *Journal of Psychoactive Drugs* 33 (2) (2001): 151–158.

63. United States Drug Enforcement Administration Press Release, 1999.

64. National Drug Threat Assessment, 2003.

65. Ibid.

# Bibliography

**Books**

Galanter, M., and H. D. Kleber. *American Psychiatric Press Textbook of Substance Abuse Treatment.* Washington, D.C.: American Psychiatric Press, 1999.

Kelly, K. *The Little Book of Ketamine.* Berkeley, CA: Ronin Publishing Inc., 1999.

Lilly, J. C. *The Scientist: A Metaphysical Autobiography.* Berkeley, CA: Ronin Publishing Inc., 1997.

Sanday, P. R. *Fraternity Gang Rape: Sex, Brotherhood, and Privilege on Campus.* New York: University Press, 1990.

Wiehe, V. R., and A. L. Richards. *Intimate betrayal: Understanding and responding to the trauma of acquaintance rape.* Thousand Oaks, CA: Sage Publications, 1995.


**Articles**

Abbey, A. "Acquaintance Rape and Alcohol Consumption on College Campuses: How Are They Linked?" *College Health* 39 (1991): 165–169.

Abbey, A., L. Thomson Ross, D. McDuggie, and P. McAuslan. "Alcohol and Dating Risk Factors for Sexual Assault among College Women." *Psychology of Women Quarterly* 20 (1996): 147–169.

Addolorato, G., E. Castelli, G. F. Stefanini, G. Casella, F. Caputo, L. Marsigli, M. Bernardi, and G. Gasbarrini. "An Open Multicentric Study Evaluating 4-hydroxybutyric Acid Sodium Salt in the Medium-term Treatment of 179 Alcohol Dependent Subjects. GHB Study Group." *Alcohol and Alcoholism* 31 (4) (1996): 341–345.

Andriamampandry, C., O. Taleb, S. Viry, C. Muller, J. P. Humbert, S. Gobaille, D. Aunis, and M. Maitre. "Cloning and Characterization of a Rat Brain Receptor that Binds the Endogenous Neuromodulator Gamma-hydroxybutyrate (GHB)." *FASEB Journal* 17 (12) (2003): 1691–1693.

Beghe, F., and M. T. Carpanini. "Safety and Tolerability of Gamma-hydroxy-butyric Acid in the Treatment of Alcohol-dependant Patients." *Alcohol* 20 (3) (2000): 223–225.

Berkowitz, A. "College Men as Perpetrators of Acquaintance Rape and Sexual Assault: A Review of Recent Research." *Journal of American College Health* 40 (1992): 175–181.

Bessman, S. P., and W. N. Fishbein. "Gamma-hydroxybutyrate: A New Metabolite in the Brain." *FASEB Journal* 22 (1963): 334.

Caldicott, D. G., and M. Kuhn. "Gamma-hydroxybutyrate Overdose and Physostigmine: Teaching New Tricks to an Old Drug?" *Annals of Emergency Medicine* 37 (1) (2001): 99–102.

Caruso, R., M. Ishikawa-Yamaki, and T. Schellenberg. "CEH Product Review: 1,4-Butanediol." *Chemical Economics Handbook.* SRI International, 1997. Available online at *http://ceh.sirc.sri.com.*

Centers for Disease Control. "Gamma Hydroxy Butyrate Use in New York and Texas, 1995–1996." *Morbidity and Mortality Weekly Report* 46 (13) (April 4, 1997).

Chin, M. Y., R. A. Kreutzer, and J. E. Dyer. "Acute Poisoning from Gamma-hydroxybutyrate in California." *Western Journal of Medicine* 156 (1992): 380–384.

Curtis, D. G. "Perspectives on Acquaintance Rape." *The American Academy of Experts in Traumatic Stress, Inc.* 1997. Available online at *http://www.aaets.org/arts/art13.htm.*

"DEA to Control 'Special K' for the First Time." Drug Enforcement Agency News Release, July 13, 1999. Available online at *http://www.usdoj.gov/dea/pubs/pressrel/pr071399.htm.*

Delgarno, P. J., and D. Shewan. "Illicit Use of Ketamine in Scotland." *Journal of Psychoactive Drugs* 28 (1996): 191–199.

Drakontides, A. B., J. A. Schneider, and W. H. Funderburk. "Some Effects of Sodium Gamma-hydroxybutyrate on the Central Nervous System." *Journal of Pharmacology and Experimental Therapeutics* 135 (1962): 275–284.

Dyer, J. E., B. Roth, and B. A. Hyma. "Gamma-hydroxybutyrate Withdrawal Syndrome." *Annals of Emergency Medicine* 37 (2001): 147–152.

Elian, A. A. "A Novel Method for GHB Detection in Urine and its Application in Drug-facilitated Sexual Assaults." *Forensic Science International* 109 (3) (2000): 183–187.

Entholzner, E., I. Mielke, R. Pichlmeier, F. Weber, and H. Seneck. "EEG Changes During Sedation with Gamma-hydroxybutyric Acid." *Anesthesiology* 44 (5) (1995): 345–350.

Fadda, F., G. Colombo, E. Mosca, and G. L. Gessa. "Suppression by Gamma-hydroxybutyric Acid of Ethanol Withdrawal Syndrome in Rats." *Alcohol and Alcoholism* 24 (1989): 447–451.

Fisher, B. S., F. T. Cullen, and M. G. Turner. "Sexual Victimization of College Women: Findings from Two National-Level Studies." Washington, D.C.: National Institute of Justice and Bureau of Justice Statistics, 2000.

# Bibliography

Gallimberti, L., G. Canton, N. Gentile, M. Ferri, M. Cibin, S. D. Ferrara, F. Fadda, and G. L. Gessa. "Gamma-hydroxybutyric Acid for Treatment of Alcohol Withdrawal Syndrome." *Lancet* 2 (8666) (1989): 787–789.

Hall, G.C.N., and R. Hirschman. "Sexual Aggression against Children: a Conceptual Perspective of Etiology." *Criminal Justice and Behavior* 19 (1992): 8–23.

Hampton, R. Y., F. Medzihradsky, J. H. Woods, and P. J. Dahlstrom. "Stereospecific Binding of $^3$H Phencyclidine in Brain Membranes." *Life Sciences* 30 (25) (1982): 2147–2154.

Hechler, V., S. Goebaille, and M. Maitre. "Selective Distribution Pattern of Gamma-hydroxybutyrate Receptors in the Rat Forebrain and Mid-brain as Revealed by Quantitative Autoradiograph." *Brain Research* 572 (1992): 345–348.

Hornfeldt, C. S., K. Lothridge, and J. C. Upshaw Downs. "Forensic Science Update: Gamma-hydroxybutyrate (GHB)." *Forensic Science Communications* 4 (2002): 1–13.

Ingels, M., C. Rangan, J. Bellezzo, and R. F. Clark. "Coma and Respiratory Depression Following the Ingestion of GHB and Its Precursors: Three Cases." *The Journal of Emergency Medicine* 19 (1) (2000): 47–50.

Jansen, K. L. "A Review of the Nonmedical use of Ketamine: Use, Users and Consequences." *Journal of Psychoactive Drugs* 32 (4) (2000): 419–433.

Jansen, K. L., and R. Darracot-Cankovic. "The Nonmedical Use of Ketamine, Part Two: A Review of Problem Use and Dependence." *Journal of Psychoactive Drugs* 33 (2) (2001): 151–158.

Karch, S. B., B. G. Stephens, and G. V. Nazareno. "GHB: Club Drug or Confusing Artifact?" *American Journal of Forensic Medicine and Pathology* 22 (3) (2001): 266–299.

Kintz, P., V. Cirimele, C. Jamey, and B. Ludes. "Testing for GHB in Hair by GC/MS/MS after a Single Exposure. Application to document sexual assault." *Journal of Forensic Science* 48 (1) (2003): 195–200.

Koss, M. P. "Hidden Rape: Sexual Aggression and Victimization in the National Sample of Students in Higher Education." *Violence in Dating Relationships: Emerging Social Issues,* eds. M. A. Pirog-Good and J. E. Stets. New York: Praeger, 1988, pp. 145–168.

Kronenberg, R. H. "Ketamine as an Analgesic: Parenteral, Oral, Rectal, Subcutaneous, Transdermal and Intranasal Administration." *Journal of Pain and Palliative Care Pharmacotherapy* 16 (3) (2002): 27–35.

Kronz, C. S. "A 30-Year-Old Woman with Possible Unknown Ingestion of Date Rape Drugs." *Journal of Emergency Nursing* 26 (2000): 544–548.

Krystal, J. H., L. P. Karper, J. P. Seibyl, G. K. Freeman, R. Delaney, J. D. Bremner, G. R. Heninger, M. B. Bowers, Jr., and D. S. Charney. "Subanesthetic Effects of the Noncompetitive NMDA Antagonist Ketamine in Humans." *Archives of General Psychiatry* 51 ( 3) (1994): 199–214.

Laborit, H. "Correlations between Protein and Serotonin Synthesis during Various Activities of the Central Nervous System (slow and desynchronized sleep, learning and memory, sexual activity, morphine tolerance, aggressiveness, and pharmacological action of sodium gamma-hydroxybutyrate)." *Research Communications in Chemical Pathology and Pharmacology* 3 (1) (1972): 58–81.

———. "Sodium 4-hydroxybutyrate." *International Journal of Neuropharmacology* 3 (1964): 433–452.

LeBeau, M. A., M. A. Montgomery, M. L. Miller, and S. G. Burmeister. "Analysis of Biofluids for Gamma-hydroxybutyrate (GHB) and Gamma-butyrolactone (GBL) by Headspace GC-FID and GC-MS." *Journal of Analytical Toxicology* 24 (6) (2000): 421–428.

Leshner, A. I. "The Essence of Drug Addiction." NIDA Publication. Available online at *http://www.drugabuse.gov/Published_Articles/Essence.html.*

Li, J., S. A. Stokes, and A. Woeckener. "A Tale of Novel Intoxication: Seven Cases of Gamma-hydroxybutyric Acid Overdose." *Annals of Emergency Medicine* 31 (1998): 723–728.

Malhotra, A. K., D. A. Pinals, H. Weingartner, K. Sirocco, C. D. Missar, D. Pickar, and A. Breier. "NMDA Receptor Function and Human Cognition: the Effects of Ketamine in Healthy Volunteers." *Neuropsychopharmacology* 14 (5) (1996): 301–307.

Mamelak, M. "Neurodegeneration, Sleep, and Cerebral Energy Metabolism: A Testable Hypothesis." *Journal of Geriatric Psychiatry and Neurology* 10 (1) (1997): 29–32.

McDowell, D. M. "MDMA, Ketamine, GHB, and the 'Club Drug' Scene." *American Psychiatric Press Textbook of Substance Abuse Treatment*, eds. M. Galanter and H. D. Kleber. Washington, D.C.: American Psychiatric Press, 1999.

Miotto, K., J. Darakjian, J. Basch, S. Murray, J. Zogg, and R. Rawson. "Gamma-hydroxybutyric Acid: Patterns of Use, Effects and Withdrawal." *American Journal of Addiction* 10 (3) (2001): 232–241.

# Bibliography

Moretti, R. J., S. Z. Hassan, L. I. Goodman, and H. Y. Meltzer. "Comparison of Ketamine and Thiopental in Healthy Volunteers: Effects on Mental Status, Mood, and Personality." *Anesthesia and Analgesia* 63 (12) (1984): 1087–1096.

Morgenthaler, J., and D. Joy. "GHB (gamma-hydroxybutyrate)." *Smart Drug News* 3 (6) (1994): 1–41.

Muehlenhard, C. L. "Misinterpreted Dating Behaviors and the Risk of Date Rape." *Violence in Dating Relationships: Emerging Social Issues*, eds. M. A. Pirog-Good and J. E. Stets. New York: Praeger, 1988, pp. 241–256.

National Drug Intelligence Center, U.S. Department of Justice. "National Drug Threat Assessment 2003." Johnstown, PA. Product No. 2003-Q0317-001. January 2003.

Nicholson, K. L., and R. L. Balster. "GHB: A New and Novel Drug of Abuse." *Drug and Alcohol Dependence* 63 (1) (2001): 1–22.

Norris, J., P. Nurius, and T. Graham. "When a Date Changes from Fun to Dangerous." *Violence Against Women* 5 (3) (1999): 230–250.

O'Connell, T., L. Kaye, and J. J. Plosay. "Gamma-hydroxybutyrate (GHB): A Newer Drug of Abuse." *American Family Physician* 62 (2000): 2478–2482.

Okun, M. S., L. A. Boothby, R. B. Bartfield, and P. L. Doering. "GHB: An Important Pharmacologic and Clinical Update." *Journal of Pharmacy and Pharmaceutical Science* 4 (2) (2001): 167–175.

O'Sullivan, C. S. "Acquaintance Gang Rape on Campus." *Acquaintance Rape: The Hidden Crime*, eds. A. Parrot and L. Bechhofer. New York: Wiley, 1991.

Palatini, R., L. Tedeschi, G. Frison, R. Padrini, R. Zordan, R. Orlando, L. Gallimberti, G. L. Gessa, and S. D. Ferrara. "Dose-dependent Absorption and Elimination of Gamma-hydroxybutyric Acid in Healthy Volunteers." *European Journal of Clinical Pharmacology* 45 (1993): 353–356.

Pan, Y. M., G. N. Gill, C. S. Tilson, W. H. Wall, and H. H. McCurdy. "Improved Procedures for the Analysis of Gamma-hydroxybutyrate and Ethylene Glycol in Whole Blood." *Journal of Analytical Toxicology* 25 (5) (2001): 328–332.

Quackenbush, R. L. "Attitudes of College Men toward Women and Rape." *Journal of College Student Development* 32 (4) (1991): 376–377.

Scharf, M. B., A. A. Lai, B. Brannigan, R. Stover, and D. B. Berkowitz. "Pharmacokinetics of Gamma-hydroxybutyrate (GHB) in Narcoleptic Patients." *Sleep* 21 (1998): 507–514.

Scrima, L., P. G. Hartman, F. H. Johnson, E. E. Thomas, and F. C. Hiller. "The Effects of Gamma-hydroxybutyrate on the Sleep of Narcolepsy Patients: A Double-blind Study." *Sleep* 13 (6) (1990): 479–490.

Shannon, M. "Toxicology Reviews: Physostigmine." *Pediatric Emergency Care* 14 (3) (1998): 224–226.

Siegel, R. K. "The Natural History of Hallucinogens." *Hallucinogens: Neurochemistry, Behavioral and Clinical Perspectives.* New York: Raven, 1984, pp. 1–18.

Simpson, D., R. A. Braithwaite, D. R. Jarvie, M. J. Stewart, S. Walker, I. W. Watson, and B. Widdop. "Screening for Drugs of Abuse (II): Cannabinoids, Lysergic Acid Diethylamide, Buprenorphine, Methadone, Barbiturates, Benzodiazepines and Other Drugs." *Annals of Clinical Biochemistry* 34 (5) (1997): 460–510.

Slaughter, L. "Involvement of Drugs in Sexual Assault." *Journal of Reproductive Medicine* 45 (2000): 425–430.

Smith, K. M., L. L. Larive, and F. Romanelli. "Club Drugs: Methylene-Dioxymethamphetamine, Flunitrazepam, Ketamine Hydrochloride and Gamma Hydroxybutyrate." *American Journal of Health System Pharmacy* 59 (2002): 1067–1076.

Staten, C. "'Roofies,' the New 'Date Rape' Drug of Choice." *Emergency Net News* 1996. Available online at *http://www.emergency.com/roofies.htm.*

Takahara, J., S. Yunoki, W. Yakushiji, J. Yamauchi, J. Yamane, and T. Ofuji. "Stimulatory Effects of Gamma-hydroxybutyric Acid on Growth Hormone and Prolactin Release in Humans." *Journal of Clinical Endocrinology and Metabolism* 44 (1977): 1014.

Tellier, P. P. "Club Drugs: Is It All Ecstasy?" *Pediatric Annals* 31 (9) (2002): 550–556.

Tobias, J. D. "Sedation and Analgesia in Paediatric Intensive Care Units: A Guide to Drug Selection and Use." *Pediatric Drugs* 1 (2) (1999): 109–126.

Tunnicliff, G. "Significance of Gamma-hydroxybutyric Acid in the Brain." *General Pharmacology* 23 (1992): 1027–1034.

———. "Sites of Actin of Gamma-hydroxybutyrate (GHB)—A Neuroactive Drug with Abuse Potential." *Journal of Toxicology and Clinical Toxicology* 35 (1997): 581–590.

Vayer, P., P. Mandel, and M. Maitre. "Gamma-hydroxybutyrate, a Possible Neurotransmitter." *Life Sciences* 41 (1987): 1547–1557.

# Bibliography

Vickers, M. D. "Gamma-hydroxybutyric Acid." *International Anesthesiology Clinics* 71 (1969): 75–89.

Vree, T. B., J. Damsma, A. G. Van den Bogert, and E. van Der Kleijn. "Pharmacokinetics of 4-hydroxybutyric Acid in Man, Rhesus Monkey and Dog." *Anaesthesiologische und Intensivmedizinische Praxis* 110 (1978): 21–39.

Walters, J. R., R. H. Roth, and G. K. Aghajanian. "Dopaminergic Neurons: Similar Biochemical and Histochemical Effects of Gamma-hydroxybutyrate and Acute Lesions of the Nigro-neostriatal Pathway." *Journal of Pharmacology and Experimental Therapeutics* 186 (1973): 630–639.

Wong, C.G.T., K. M. Gibson, and O. C. Snead. "From the Street to the Brain: Neurobiology of the Recreational Drug Gamma-hydroxybutyric Acid." *Trends in Pharmacological Sciences* 25 (1) (2004): 29–34.


## Websites
**American Council for Drug Education**
*www.acde.org*

**American Society of Addiction Medicine**
*www.asam.org*

**Association for Medical Education and Research in Substance Abuse**
*www.fda.gov/cder*

**Community Epidemiology Work Group (CEWG)**
*www.drugabuse.gov/about/organization/CEWG/CEWGHome.html*

**Drug Abuse Warning Network (DAWN)**
*dawninfo.samhsa.gov*

**Monitoring the Future (MTF)**
*www.monitoringthefuture.org*
*www.monitoringthefuture.org/pubs/monographs/vol1_2002.pdf*

**National Drug Threat Assessment Survey**
*www.usdoj.gov/ndic/pubs3/3300/3300p.pdf*

**National Institute on Drug Abuse (NIDA)**
*www.drugabuse.gov*
*www.nida.nih.gov*

**Office of National Drug Control Policy**

*www.whitehousedrugpolicy.gov*
*www.whitehousedrugpolicy.gov/publications/factsht/rohypnol/index.html*
   (Rohypnol)

**Pulse Check**

*www.whitehousedrugpolicy.gov/drugfact/pulsecheck.html*

**Substance Abuse and Mental Health Services Administration**

*www.samhsa.gov*
*www.findtreatment.samhsa.gov*

**U.S. Drug Enforcement Administration**

*www.dea.gov*

# Further Reading

## Books

Carter, Christine, ed. *The Other Side of Silence: Women Tell About Their Experiences With Date Rape.* Gilsum, NH: Avocus Publishing, 1997.

Kelly, K. *The Little Book of Ketamine.* Berkeley, CA: Ronin Publishing Inc., 1999.

Robinson, Fran. *It Didn't Happen.* Victoria, British Columbia, Canada: Trafford, 2003.

Sanday, P. R. *Fraternity Gang Rape: Sex, Brotherhood, and Privilege on Campus.* New York: University Press, 1990.

Tattersall, Claire. *Date Rape Drugs.* New York: Rosen, 2000.

Warshaw, Robin. *I Never Called It Rape: The Ms. Report on Recognizing, Fighting, and Surviving Date and Acquaintance Rape.* New York: Perennial, 1994.

Wiehe, V. R., and A. L. Richards. *Intimate Betrayal: Understanding and Responding to the Trauma of Acquaintance Rape.* Thousand Oaks, CA: Sage Publications; 1995.

## Websites

**American Council for Drug Education**
*www.acde.org*

**Association for Medical Education and Research in Substance Abuse**
*dawninfo.samhsa.gov/*

**Monitoring the Future (MTF)**
*www.monitoringthefuture.org*
*www.monitoringthefuture.org/pubs/monographs/vol1_2002.pdf*

**National Drug Threat Assessment Survey**
*www.usdoj.gov/ndic/pubs3/3300/3300p.pdf*

**National Institute on Drug Abuse (NIDA)**
*www.drugabuse.gov*
*www.nida.nih.gov*

**Office of National Drug Control Policy**
*www.whitehousedrugpolicy.gov*
*www.whitehousedrugpolicy.gov/publications/factsht/rohypnol/index.html*
(Rohypnol)

**Substance Abuse and Mental Health
    Services Administration**
*www.samhsa.gov*
*www.findtreatment.samhsa.gov*

**U.S. Drug Enforcement Administration**
*www.dea.gov*

# Index

# Picture Credits

page:

17: Associated Press, AP
21: Lambda Science Artwork
22: Courtesy of the DEA
51: AP Graphics

57: Lambda Science Artwork
58: Courtesy of the DEA
60: Lambda Science Artwork

# About the Author

**George B. Kehner, Ph.D.** is an Assistant Professor of Pharmacology at Temple University School of Medicine in Philadelphia, Pennsylvania. He obtained his doctoral degree in pharmacology from Temple University and earned his B.S. degree in Biology from St. Joseph's University. Dr. Kehner is a member of the College on Problems of Drug Dependence and is an active lecturer and researcher in the field of drug abuse.

# About the Editor

**David J. Triggle** is a University Professor and a Distinguished Professor in the School of Pharmacy and Pharmaceutical Sciences at the State University of New York at Buffalo. He studied in the United Kingdom and earned his B.Sc. degree in Chemistry from the University of Southampton and a Ph.D. degree in Chemistry at the University of Hull. Following post-doctoral work at the University of Ottawa in Canada and the University of London in the United Kingdom, he assumed a position at the School of Pharmacy at Buffalo. He served as Chairman of the Department of Biochemical Pharmacology from 1971 to 1985 and as Dean of the School of Pharmacy from 1985 to 1995. From 1995 to 2001 he served as the Dean of the Graduate School, and as the University Provost from 2000 to 2001. He is the author of several books dealing with the chemical pharmacology of the autonomic nervous system and drug-receptor interactions, some 400 scientific publications, and has delivered over 1,000 lectures worldwide on his research.